SCENES AND THOUGHTS

IN

EUROPE.

BY

GEORGE H. CALVERT.

SECOND SERIES.

NEW YORK:
GEORGE P. PUTNAM, 10 PARK PLACE.

1852.

Entered, according to Act of Congress, in the year 1852,
BY GEORGE H. CALVERT,
In the Clerk's Office of the Southern District of New York.

CONTENTS.

CHAPTER I.

CHAPTER II.

CHAPTER III.

CHAPTER IV.

CHAPTER V.

CHAPTER VI.

CHAPTER VII.

CHAPTER VIII.

CHAPTER IX.

CHAPTER X.

CHAPTER XI.

CHAPTER XII.

CHAPTER XIII.

CHAPTER XIV.

CHAPTER XV.

CHAPTER XVI.

CHAPTER XVII.

CHAPTER XVIII.

CHAPTER XIX.

CHAPTER XX.

SCENES AND THOUGHTS IN EUROPE.

CHAPTER I.

THE RHINE—BINGEN—WIESBADEN.

To be taken up by a steamboat on the Rhine is always a lively incident. Out from her level path to the pier the strenuous gay boat glides with a grace that captivates the traveller, like the smiling welcome of a beautiful hostess. On the morning of Monday the 22d of July, 1850, there was a fog on the river, so that the *Goethe*, due at Boppart at half-past one, did not arrive from Coblenz till past two. Seated on the quay with cheerful company, we escaped the vacuum which, to the idle as well as to the busy, ever comes with waiting.

To be ushered of a sudden, hungry, upon the scene of a repast that has been, with the fragments of good cheer strewn around, is not a happy beginning. When we got on board dinner was over. Under the awning, at the long, narrow tables, with tall, empty Rhenish bottles in the midst, a medley of nations were chatting German, French, English, with the volubility and complacency of satisfied appetites.

Man is the creature of food. To be well fed is the first condition of thriving manhood. Let the others take rank as they may, this is the basis. The British tar was right, who, on seeing the beef destined for an American man-of-war, exclaimed, "D—— 'em, no wonder they fight so." Let Europe look to it. The twenty-five millions of the United States take in daily as much nutriment as almost double the number of any other Christian feeders. Not that the Americans are overfed: the Europeans are fearfully underfed. John Bull is getting puzzled and alarmed at the pace at which Jonathan is "going ahead." Let him bethink him, that while to his millions roast beef is a tradition or a festival, to ours it or its equivalent is a daily smoking reality. Democracy and "a good bellyful" go together. The which takes precedence as cause, we will not now stop to determine. Our well-being depends primarily upon what we eat. Nature ordains that man should feed well, plenteously, variously. To mortify the flesh, except to counterbalance a surfeit, is a sacrilege and an impertinence.

Reflections like these come up, without forcing, from an empty stomach into the brain of a man waiting for his dinner.

I had not talked three minutes with my neighbor at the table before he brought in California. Neither the resumption of payment by defaulting States, nor the feats of the Mexican war, have raised us in European esteem so much as the possession of California. Virtue with the Romans meant courage, it now means cash. If men were not hypocrites they would call the Rothschilds the most virtuous family in Europe. California is in everybody's thought and mouth. Gold! gold! Protean potentate, flexible omnipotence, gentle conqueror—what can it, what can it not? By giving it, we get peace within and good-will without; by lending it, gratitude and six per cent.; by promising it, the service of the strong; by spending it, profit or pleasure; by hoarding it, we have the more of it, and by having it we are masters of most that the world prizes. He who speaks contemptuously of gold is a dissembler or a simpleton.

—— The Rhine, fatted by the maternal glaciers of Switzerland, rushes down resistless, like a headlong herd of buffaloes on a prairie. But we drive steadily up, and heed not his torrent, taming his counter-flood to our will with the wizard hand of

Genius. How divine, to wrest from the great heart of Nature a pregnant secret, and endow the world with a new force, immeasurable, infinite. The boats on the Rhine have good fitting names, but not one of them the best and fittest, the name of Fulton.—I look up, and above the modern landscape, still cresting his vine-mantled hill, a stern old ruin paints his jagged outline on the sunny sky, and brags of the past, like some weather-beaten grand-papa. At the water's edge the blackened broken wall fences in part the compact little town, from whose midst rises the bulky church, triste, heavy, unsightly from without; triste, chill, prosaic within; where mechanical priests still drive their huckstering trade, selling what they have not earned, and cannot possess without earning, fuddling the green imaginations with doctrinal strong-waters, compressing the expansive intellect, paralyzing the vivid soul, frightening to subject, enlarging themselves to belittle the multitude, whom they darken where they should enlighten; thus blaspheming while they affect to pray. The churches that arose under the inspiration of Beauty, the which it is a joy and an exaltation to behold, are as rare as are the spiritually-entitled priests, whom it is a privilege to hear.

—— As you stand on the heights in its rear, Bingen smiles up to you, enwreathed with vineyards,—Bacchanal Bingen. The precious, petted vines,—just now in their pride of leaf and fresh luxuriance of new juicy shoots,—press up to the walls, and over them into the town itself. Opposite, Rudesheim piles its fruitful terraces, and a little further is Geisenheim, and beyond Johanisberg,—inspiring names, that stand high and highest on the scroll that the traveller pores over with daily renewed zest. All around is one green wine-promising abundance.

The happiest eyes that from the deck of the boat gazed upon the warm, expanded landscape between Bingen and Biberich, were those of a German, naturalized in the United States, and revisiting, after ten years' absence, his native Germany. The man seemed to feel for the first time, in all its fulness, the sweet strength of his new ties. The joy of rebeholding the land of his birth disclosed to him the intensity of his love for the land of his adoption. Of what "we" had and did in America he spoke with the glow of one who had been raised to a new dignity. As watching the mellow shifting landscape, we talked of America, his countenance beamed with a compound delight. Through the present enjoyment shone the deeper satisfaction of thoughts that were busied with his new home. There, in democratic America, he had been reborn and rebaptized. He was conscious that he had become a larger, abler man than he could have been in Germany. He could not conceal his happiness, that he had exchanged a home that was so dear to him for one that was still dearer.

—— Wiesbaden owes its summer life to two poisons,—its boiling mineral spring, and its ravenous roulette-tables. Early in the morning, round the "Koch-Brunnen" (boiling spring) a motley crowd of pallid dupes cool their smoking glasses to below the scalding point, credulously abiding the sulphurous self-infliction of repeated seething draughts. In the evening, a denser throng encircle in eager morbid silence the gaming-tables, where rich and poor, men and women, sick and well, fascinated by the gloating eye of Mammon, throw their tens and thousands into the monster's maw. On one of the few days that we stopped at Wiesbaben, a rich banker lost in a single evening four thousand pounds sterling. I was told of another player whose eyebrows turned white in a few days after continued heavy losses.

These crowded summer resorts represent the pursuit of pleasure under difficulties.

CHAPTER II.

HEIDELBERG—SUNSET—PRUSSIAN SOLDIERY.

Could a man be said to have travelled from Dan to Beersheba, who had compassed the space between the two by steam? Travelling implies effort, a concurrent locomotive activity, and a self-guidance on the part of the traveller. Once in a railroad car, he is passive, subordinated, without will or authority, with but even a tatter of personality left to him, in the shape of his ticket. He doesn't travel, he is transported, and is hurriedly thrust out on the platform of a station, just as though, instead of being a bag of electrified capillaries, he were but a bag of oats. In this way we came in a few hours from Wiesbaden to Heidelberg.

The beautiful structures of man's making rise from the earth like a favored growth out of it. They are adopted by Nature. The sun rejoices to shine on them. The Castle of Heidelberg we reached in time to behold it by a sunset of American gorgeousness. The rosy atmosphere deepened the expression of the beautiful inward façade which stood again before us, ever young and fresh. Perennial youth is not a fable, or a futile longing: it is the gift of Genius to its handiwork, and is the touchstone of Art. But a work of genuine art is not only young itself,—it makes you young. To revisit it, annihilates time. The intervening years are bridged over by a rainbow.

Through time-rents and vacant casements the rich horizontal beams fell with a glow of celestial gladness. From the terrace, the town beneath, with the valley and plain that stretched far away towards the burning west, lay in a blissful tranquillity. Alas! only to the outward eye, bribed by the purple opulence of light. In this seeming Paradise the ubiquitous Serpent is at work, and here is neither bliss nor peace, but in their stead, unrest, misery. This magnificent leave-taking between Sun and Earth, this illuminated farewell, this broad parting look of love, which lights up the countenance of the responsive Earth with an intense flush of beauty,—how many see it or share it, of the tens of thousands there below, on whom it falls? In torpid imbecility, in exasperated conflict, they lie and writhe there, with senses closed to the eloquent heavenly message. This beauty, which is for them, they cannot claim; this magnificence of nature, they are too poor to accept. The few who, by fortune or spiritual effort, possess freedom enough to enjoy, revel on such spectacles, and in them escape from the omnivorous evil around, their imaginations purged by this transfiguring light. Only for a moment they escape, for the ghastly realities can be but momentarily laid. Not as the evanescent demons of a dream do these come, but as the abiding terrors that leap upon the awakening criminal. So begirt are we by implacable hostilities; self-doomed to have every joy shadowed by a sorrow, every love dogged by a hate, every possession haunted by a fear.

Descending into the town, we came upon squads of Prussian soldiery. Whenever I meet these mechanized men, these soul-informed machines, these man-shaped irresponsibilities, I feel saddened, humiliated, insulted. Plainer than words they say to me,—speak not, think not, act not. In their presence I am utterly quenched. I feel myself supplanted, and in my place a musket. In their speechless tramp there is somethimg terrific. This steeled silence controls my speech: this noiseless movement paralyzes my will.

The European armies hang on the nations, a monstrous idleness, a universal polluting scab. In them are condensed into one vast blight the seven plagues of Egypt. Like the "frogs," they "come upon the people, into their houses, their bed-chambers, their ovens, their kneading-troughs." How this picture fits them in all its traits. Look at those knots of lounging dirty soldiers: they swarm and buzz over the whole land, like the "lice and flies," only more befouling than these. Are they not "sores and blains" on the people, a moral and physical corruption, and a drain upon their strength? "The fire that ran along on the ground"—what could realize it more vividly than the march of armies, smiting like the "hail" as they pass, both man and beast, and herb and tree, and eating like the "locusts" the fruits of the earth and every green thing. In the crowning "Plague of Darkness," the likeness is the most palpable. Standing armies are the very fomenters of darkness. Their office is to propagate night and make men sleep on. They are coarse, brutalizing Force, in contrast and conflict with the subtle, humanizing, liberating power of the intellect and heart of man. They are a million-mouthed extinguisher plied ceaselessly by the hand of Despotism, to crush out the light so fast as it jets up. They exist to enforce man's law against God's law, to be the jailers of thought, the executioners of freedom.

CHAPTER III.

THE NECKAR—STUTTGARDT—ULM—NAPOLEON.

Going up the valley of the Neckar, one runs over with impracticable desires, and their tantalizing importunity is an index of the overflowing abundance of its beauties. How many sites that one longs to halt at for a day; how many hills that one would climb, to compass a wider enjoyment. But we must be at Heilbron in time to dine, before taking the railroad to Stüttgardt. To no one is dinner a more important item in the day's account than to your traveller.

Stüttgardt is a "Residenz." A "Residenz" is a German town, lifted into consequence from its being chosen by the sovereign of a petty dominion for the residence of his petty self and his petty court. In the body-politic of Germany, these reiterated capitals assume to be ganglia, or nervous centres, whence political vitality (so much as there may be) is diffused through the little circle upon each dependant. They are absorbents rather, and of a wen-like turgescence, seeing that they suck in, as well of spiritual force as of material substance, more than they impart. Here, in a small theatre, is performed, without interlude, the serio-comedy of Kingship, wherein Usurpation brazens it out by a prescription of impudence, and Servility is so low that it knows not its own lowness; where the emptiest actors play often the highest parts; and where the audience is terribly out at elbows, being forced to forego, most of them, even some of the necessaries of a meagre household, to furnish the gilded trappings of the performers. To an American, there is no more astonishing feature in European existence, than the patience of the people. Their forbearance is to me a daily marvel.

—— Railroads lay open the landscapes of a country; they take to the valleys. At Geislingen, between Stüttgardt and Ulm, there is one of rare beauty, which, before you issue out of its upper end, narrows to a gorge, where the ascent achieved being of several hundred feet, the delight of the traveller is redoubled by admiration of man's mechanical art. With noiseless ease the heavy train rolls up the valley. True power is so unostentatious. I know not a clearer image, at once of might and beneficence than a silent shower, that slakes the thirst of half a continent. Witnessing it, one wonders at the large facility of Nature. A great idea or discovery, offspring of the prolific brain of man, works and fertilizes with a like breadth and bounty.

—— Ulm is historical. It is one of the many Continental towns branded with notoriety by the fatal hand of Napoleon. It was here, in 1805, while Europe awaited with breathless intentness his descent upon England, that Napoleon, sped by his demoniacal instincts, having rapidly traversed France from Boulogne to Strasburg, suddenly faced the astounded Austrians, cut in two their force, and by the capture of sixty thousand men at Ulm, opened the campaign, which in a few weeks was to end with the victory of Austerlitz.

What grasping thoughts now swelled that vivid brain, making even the new diadem too small for it. As on the daily outspread chart the sure eye of the General tracked the marches of the enemy, the Imperial glance ranged far beyond the lines of a campaign, and kindling with dark power, devoured land after land on the broad map of Europe. Between him and his hope, no majestic figure of Justice, no tearful countenance of Humanity uprose to rebuke his desires. The higher his eminence, the less he felt the wants of his fellows. As he ascended, he put away from him more and more the nobler attributes of man's nature; until, at the culmination of his path, he had become an icy ambition-mastered inhumanity, illuminated by intellect.

He was now rapidly mounting. From the height gained by the victory at Ulm, his horizon widened of a sudden. Into the future he glared with exultation. The foes before him he felt were his prey. He strode on to clutch them. Munich he entered as a deliverer. Elated with conquest, exalted by Bavarian homage, flushed with ambitious visions, the new Emperor seized in his audacious thought a boundless sovereignty.—A courier arrives from the west. What brings he? A tremor seizes Napoleon's frame. His face is livid. His lurid eye rolls, as though tortured by the brain behind it. Fled are those gigantic visions. Far away from the Austrian are his thoughts. He writhes with anger and hate. In his hand is the report of the battle of Trafalgar.

Napoleon has himself said, that but for the obstinate resistance of Sir Sidney Smith at Acre, the course of history had been changed. From the beginning to the end of his career he was baffled by the sturdy Islanders. This was part of his "Destiny." At Acre; at the Nile; at Trafalgar; at Copenhagen, where their seizure of the Danish fleet, disconcerted again his plans, and poured gall into the brimming cup of his German triumphs; in Spain, where he boasted that he would drive that Sepoy (Wellington) into the Atlantic. At the high tides of his affairs came ever this adverse potency to make an ebb in his fortunes. When his fortunes had waned, it was England that gave, at Waterloo, the finishing blow, and then bound the Imperial Upstart to a far rock in the tropical ocean, there to be slowly devoured by the vulture of his own sensations.

This strength to master the giant, England drew from her freedom. The Continental States were all Despotisms. One after the other they fell before democratized France. Napoleon, a child of the Revolution, wielded its fiery vigor to crush the old tyrannies. His own new one he set up in their stead. He cheated France of her revolutionary earnings. In exchange for the gold of political rights, he gave her the gilt copper of military glory. Her people were again effaced before his will. She became a new despotism amid old despotisms. She was shorn of half her new strength. England was the only great nation where the People were for something in the State. Like Austria and Russia, she had made war against Napoleon for self-preservation; but unlike them she never succumbed to the despot. But for her, they would have been his subordinate fellow-despots. In her the feeling of national independence was kept erect by the breath of freedom. Napoleon, who would that no one had a will but himself, who hated any and every man's liberty, who strove to centre in himself all political vitality, who sucked the French nation dry of its liberal juices, felt that England, the only home for freedom in Europe, was his most dread foe. He struck at her with his whole might; but her might, nurtured by liberty, was stronger than his, poisoned by slavery. Thus, his very power became his weakness. In his prosperity, he had absorbed into himself the life-blood of France: in his adversity, he found himself the head of a corpse.

The Emperor of Russia takes the place of Bonaparte in hatred of England. Russia would rule Europe through despotism. National rivalries are not barriers enough to check her. Austria as a State, has the most to dread from Russia; and yet they are, through the paramount necessities of despotism, fast allies.

In the struggle between regal governments, backed by autocratic Russia, and the governed, or more properly the misgoverned, led by France, aristocratic England must back the Peoples. And this, not alone ambitiously to thwart Russian ambition, but from the deep instincts of her national being, whose health and strength spring from the democratic element in her

Constitution. This makes her the political enemy of Russia and Austria, and at the same time gives her the force to withstand them. The intensity of life and the resources of a nation, are in proportion to the political participation of the people.* Therefore it is, that in Europe, England ranks first in wealth and power. Therefore, the United States,—who left behind them in their nest the impure political principles, the monarchical and the aristocratic, and carried with them only the pure principle, the democratic—have grown with such astounding rapidity, that already, within three generations, in intrinsic resources they take the lead of England, their European mother, and who alone could have been their mother. In this conflict between Peoples and Princes, between Right and Wrong, between Light and Darkness, shall it become necessary for Democratic America to intervene, otherwise than with the daily influence of her principles and her example, let the strongest beware.

By the having achieved a larger liberty than has yet been enjoyed, we march in the van of all the nations of the Earth. With us, humanity unfolds itself in broader, deeper strata. Liberty cannot but purify, enlarge, invigorate. It harbors an inevitable, an involuntary virtue. Even martial conquests it transmutes into beneficences. Thus, where we conquer, we emancipate. Our taking possession is not an enthralment, but a deliverance. We cannot subjugate, we must elevate.

* So morbid is their condition, that in European States there are two divided constituents,—the governing and the governed, the privileged and the despoiled. Only to the latter, that is, the laborers, the *vile multitude*, as M. Thiers calls them, is now applied the generic term, the People. With us there is but one constituent: we are all People.

CHAPTER IV.

LAKE OF CONSTANCE—SWITZERLAND—LAKE OF THUN—THE YUNGFRAU—LAUTERBRUNNEN—THE WENGERN ALP.

From Ulm the railroad carries you in a few hours to Friedrichshafen, on the Lake of Constance. This is one of the best routes for entering Switzerland. You come upon it suddenly. The transition from plain to mountain is across the Lake, whose level expanse magnifies the contrast. You get out of the cars and find yourself in the sublime presence. Just over the clear water, quite near, is the strange land, that leaves the earth and goes up into the air, a land built into the heavens. It looked like a discovery.

When the sun shines, travelling in Switzerland is a perpetual festival. Mother Earth holds here a jubilee. She welcomes her children with the laughter of water-falls, the thunder of avalanches, the smiles of green valleys, the salutations of towering granite, the gaze of snow-glistened peaks. You share the sublime joy that beams from her countenance. Your soul and senses expand to be in accord with her grandeurs. You are magnified by the magnificence around you. Nature here pours out her generic power in floods. She is in a mood of Titanic revelry. She leaps and shouts. The Earth is heaved up and down in exuberance of beauty, so inundated is matter by creative spirit.

—— On the 18th of August, 1850, the clouds, that for days had darkened the Lake of Thun, and hidden all save the bases of the nearest mountains, lifted their compact curtain of sombre vapor, let in light upon the Lake, turned up their broken masses to be dried and whitened by the sun, and re-opened to the grateful eye the far-shining snow-peaks of the Yungfrau. A good day, like a good deed, makes you forget a score of bad ones.

At two the little steamboat, with its freight of cheerful tourists, issued from the port of Thun for its afternoon voyage to the eastern end of the Lake. The deep water, like a deep heart, took in and gave back from its tranquil surface the grandeurs and beauties about it. The mountains and the vapory mimicries of them built in the air, painted themselves with the warm light into the depths of the Lake, breaking and beautifying with their images its liquid level. Before us, to the right, the far Blumlis peaks of eternal snow shone whitely among the clouds that they had gathered about them as a foil to their own whiteness. Looking back when half-way up the Lake, the Niessen, that rises from the water's edge a regular pyramid a mile high with a base equal to its height, presented a magnificent spectacle. To one side and round the head of the mountain, an isolated, dark mass of cloud clung with a mysterious, threatening look, as though, blackened by anger, it would wrestle with it as with a foe. The sunbeams behind, that seemed to issue up from the Earth, illuminating one edge of the black cloud, added to the splendor of the effect. A little later the cloud had risen, and shrouding just the peak of the mountain, gave it the aspect of a volcano in travail.

The Lake being ten miles long, we landed in an hour, and soon had our faces turned southward towards the Valley of Lauterbrunnen. From the hot plain of Interlachen, beyond and above the high angle formed by the interlapping green mountains of the narrow valley, the Yungfrau shone a dazzling front of white, clear and palpable, yet dreamy and unreal, from its unearthlike beauty. Of the snowy surface, the eye, from this point, takes in probably a mile square, a wall of solid white two miles up in the air, bounded below by the outline of mountains, in the inverted angle of which it seems to rest. It was like an abstraction, a sublimated essence of the Earth; so calm, so pure, out of common reach, up-piercing, predominating. Like a high abstraction too, infolding the condensed substance of truth—which it cherishes and widely imparts, to the enrichment of many and distant minds—those pre-eminent white peaks are inexhaustible fertilizers, sending down from their heavenly elevation food for great rivers. In Nature there is no waste, nothing useless or idle. Everything works. Everything has its life, its purpose, its dependence interlocked with its power. The distant flats of Holland feel the power of this cold pinnacle of the Yungfrau, which helps to keep full the freighted channel of the Rhine; while on the rivers that she feeds she is herself dependent, the impalpable exhalations from them, condensed in the upper air, furnishing the snow, which in her sublime strength she sends back in avalanches, that give to the torrents, born in her bosom, the volume and speed to hurry to the plain. On her summit the Creative Spirit is enthroned in unspeakable grandeur, and works thence with a ceaseless bounty.

We were soon inclosed in the wonderful valley, whose sides are steep fir-clad mountains, or perpendicular planes of bare rock a quarter of a mile high. Down its stony path, the Lutchine, whose source is in the near glaciers, comes shouting fiercely, as it were the bearer of an angry message from the mountains.

At the village of Lauterbrunnen, our resting-place for the night, is the brook which falls into the valley over a precipice nine hundred feet high, and thence, from being shivered into spray by the wind and the height of its fall, gets the name of Dustbrook (Staubach). Itself a wonder, it is a type of this valley of wonders. From the twilight below, we beheld, over the green mountains, the rosy sunset that bloomed for several minutes on one of the snowy peaks. It was like a glimpse into a brighter world.

The next morning at half-past five, my young companion and myself, well mounted, were on our way up the Wengern Alp. The cool clear air gave us a good appetite for a bad breakfast at the inn near the top, which we reached at eight.

Now we are face to face with the white giantess, between us a deep, black chasm. We stand a mile above the sea level, and even with us is the snow-line of the *Yungfrau*. The summit is more than two miles above the sea; so that we have, right in front and above us, distant from one to two thousand yards, and seeming but a few hundred, a mass of vertical snow more than a mile high, and several in breadth. The eye strives to grow familiar with these sublimities. Far below are all sounds of the common Earth. About us is a sublime silence, so wide and deep, that nothing small can break it; common noises only scratch its surface; it is broken by the avalanche. This solid, up-stretching, white immensity! This mountain-measured distance! This unearthly silence! This thunder-voice of the avalanche! Nothing is ordinary and every-day-like but the sunshine. We heard and saw several avalanches. They look like a fall of water, and sound like a roar of thunder. Over the chasm an eagle is circling.

Before noon we were again on the road to Gründelwald. As we advanced we had in view successively, and at times several or all together, the *Yungfrau*, the *Monck*, the *Eiger*, the *Wetterhorn*, the *Schreckhorn*, and the *Finster-Aarhorn* the least of them more than 13,000 feet above the sea-level, and the *Aarhorn*, the highest of the sublime group, over 14,000. What company for a morning ride! We passed the relics of a forest blasted by avalanches, and far down the descent a patch of snow. At Gründelwald we visited one of the glaciers—a huge, creeping, Saurian monster, with its tail high up among the eternal snows, its body prostrate in a rocky gorge, and its head flattened upon the green valley, into which it was spouting turbid water.

CHAPTER V.

MOUNTAINEERS—ISOLATION—PRACTICAL ART—MAN'S AGENTS—PRINCES AND PRIESTS —SACERDOTAL DESPOTISM—CATHOLICISM—JESUITISM—CONCLUSIONS.

MOUNTAINEERS cannot but be hardy. They have a constant fight with Nature to win a livelihood. The stern, fixed features of their abode limit their being, and give to it a one-sided intensity. From these causes they are courageous, independent, with a strong, fond clinging to their home. Witness the Swiss, the Caucasians, the Highlanders of Scotland. At the same time, from being isolated and confined, they are inflexible and stationary. Dogged, persevering, tough, they are not expansive, not progressive.

Isolation withers whether man or community. The first need for human growth is contact. The closer, wider, more varied the contact, the stronger, fuller, straighter will be the growth. Heeren says justly, that a great source of Phenician, Grecian, Roman development was the Mediterranean. Besides its practical facilities, a sea acts healthfully on the mind by motion and fluidity, inviting its capabilities, giving it a broad impulse. Here is an immensity, and yet to be compassed,—a boundlessness, and yet to be explored. The Swiss want this ever-urgent opportunity of expansion. Their geographical completes their political isolation, their country being withal circumscribed. The very sublimities of their land are practically a hindrance, rather than a furtherance. These awful heights do not lift up, they press down the people. These grand glaciers feed the Rhine and the Rhone and the Tessino, for the use of others. The centres of Swiss culture are away from proximity with avalanches and precipices, in the midst of warm arable fields, at Zürich and Geneva, near the frontiers of Germany and France.

A rugged, ungenerous soil, inland, cannot rear a strong people. Scotland and New England could not have nurtured so thorough a breed, but for having at their door the land-embracing ocean. Through it, the whole world, open to their enterprise, is made tributary to their invention. For development, nations need the sea. The ancients had the Mediterranean. Since that the earth has grown larger, and nations with it. The Atlantic is now the Mediterranean. Soon all the oceans will form but one Mediterranean for all the continents—a universal path for intercommunication among all the peoples.

——With an ever deeper embrace Art encircles her elder sister, Nature; the two co-working with man for his deliverance. The highest service of practical Art is, to bring men together. For this, greater instruments are needed in the modern enlarged field, than in the ancient confined one. Types, steam, electricity, these are the mighty modern instruments. They are at once the signs and means of elevation. They are cause after having been effect.* They denote moral as well as intellectual activity; for in productive action there is always virtue. The most selfish workers carry forward undesignedly the common cause.

* These great tools are but growths, elongations of the intellect,—helps, which in its fulness it contrives for itself. All machines are but man-made fingers, legs, eyes, ears. Thence, the mind that has not swelled to the want of them, cannot use them. What are types or the telescope in the hands of the savage? And thence, the degree of activity wherewith those tools are plied, marks the rank of nations in the scale of humanity. Pass from the heart of Russia to the heart of England, from the sterile animalism of Africa to the affluent humanity of America. In Africa, types and steam are unknown; in Russia they are still in embryo; in England and America, to arrest them for a day, were to arrest and confuse the great currents of life.

Life is movement. On the earth man is the centre of life. For invigorating, multiplying, beautifying life, all Nature is at his service. At first he uses partially, grossly, passively, only her palpable simple qualities. Compare the tools, and the work done with them, of the savage, with the tools and work of the civilized.

The subtler his agents, the larger is man's gain of power. Who can compute what he has gained by steam? Enter a crowded capital by night, to learn what a centupled flood of light comes from an imponderable substance. What are battering-rams to gunpowder, whose terrible force is in the sudden liberation of a gas. Subtler than either, electricity,—now our postman,—has a speed which cannot be calculated. Subtlest of all, master of them all, clutching their combined force in its grasp, out-shining the sun, out-running the electric flash, in resources infinite, in power immeasurable, is the mind of man! the centre, summit and consummation of earthly being, the quintessence of things, the jewel of the world, the citadel of humanity, the final superlative in Nature,—the boundless receptacle, the exhaustless source, whither and whence, backward and forward, flow the streams of the multiplex movement which we call the world,—the mystic womb of thought, in whose vast depths lie the Past, the Present, the Future,—the mighty generator, who on earth generates all the deeds of men, and with man-like shapes peoples the infinite beyond,—the dauntless seeker, who on the dread confines of being confronts the Creative Spirit of the Universe, and wrestles with him for his secrets.

This divine fire, who dare wish to quench or control it? The sacrilegious, who would handle this sublime essence as they do gas and steam, who are they? They are Princes and Priests.

In the beginning, natural superiorities are readily acknowledged. By their sympathies not less than by their weaknesses, men yield to guidance. So long as it is guidance and not direction, so long as real superiority is the condition of leadership, the relation between guides and guided is healthy. But in the imperfect social organizations, for the elastic play of natural tendencies, is soon substituted the rigid pressure of artificial arrangements. Men invent laws, instead of discovering them. Then humanity is turned awry. Then in place of impartiality and freedom and natural growth, there is—in proportion to the rigidity of the conventional ordinances—one-sidedness, compression, tyranny. The human-arbitrary takes place of the divine-free. Willingly or not, men have abdicated their native sovereignty; there is enforced submission; they are governed, ruled, commanded. Their strength has passed away from them, to be centered in a caste, a class, a family. Above them, in permanent possession, absorbing their wills, controlling their thoughts, ordering their acts, are irresponsible masters, greedy monopolists of power. Scorning men, defying God, jealous, self-seeking, unsympathizing, the first objects of the suspicion, envy, wrath, of these self-constituted, unhallowed leaders, are the men commissioned by Nature to be the guides of humanity. The mission of these is to enlighten, to exalt; the aim of the former is to domineer over, to possess men. The inspired benefactors, the parents of new thoughts, the revealers and champions of great truths—they who are endowed with genius to vivify and enlarge the minds of their fellows, when they have not ended a life of persecution by the cross or the fagot, have mostly lived unacknowledged to die unregretted.

Two hundred years ago, a tribunal of Theologians sitting in Rome, pronounced the assertion, that *the earth moves*, to be not only heretical in religion, but absurd in philosophy; and to the assertor applied the rack to extort a retraction of this truth, which his genius had revealed in its high communings with God. More presumptuous, more blasphemous than the angry denial of the movement of the earth, is the denial of the movement of the human mind. The same tribunal still sits in Rome, and to its officials in all quarters of the globe proclaims, that in matters the most vital,—his duty to God, his duty to his fellows,—judgment shall not unfold itself in the brain of man, but be passively accepted from this tribunal, the privileged fabricator of religious and moral laws. This inhuman, this godless proclamation, it endeavors to enact by means adapted to the condition of each land; by the gaol and gibbet in priest-rotten Italy,—by gilded sophistries, by feigned pliancy, by Judas-kisses in Protestant America.

Of all despotism, the sacerdotal is the most desolating, both its end and means being the direct subjection of the mind. Irresponsible priests are worse enemies of mankind than princes. Hating each other as rival usurpers, with an unchristian hate, they have from necessity mostly leagued together to bemaster the intellect and soul; believing, that he who could possess himself of the minds of men, would own the treasure of treasures. But the selfish are ever short-sighted. It is seldom given to thieves to enjoy their thefts. When priests have robbed their brother of that which makes him poor indeed, the wealth that he has lost enricheth not the robber; for, by a deep law of Nature, which decrees the inviolability of the human soul, the moment the mind is invaded it ceases to be a treasure. The contiguous breath of the possessor bedims the splendor of the jewel. Freedom gives the only light by which it sparkles. In subjection, the mind pines and perishes. On itself must it be poised, out of itself draw its life, within itself must be its supreme tribunal. Else it has no spring for elevation, no self-renewing vitality, no self-rectifying force. It languishes, it sickens, it dwindles. But not alone. They who on the holy of holies lay impious hands, the Cains who kill their brothers' souls, they dwindle with it; they become little with the littleness they have caused. Look at Spain, at Portugal, at Italy, the People and their Priests. What an intellectual wilderness! What children are the People, what wet and dry nurses their pastors!

Rome being the centre of Catholicism, in the upper ranks of the Hierarchy there, an intellectual activity is maintained by the conflict thence directed against Protestantism in the freer countries of Christendom. No correspondent moral activity is visible. On the contrary, being predominant, absolute, irresponsible, living in isolated grandeur high above the people, the upper clergy in Rome is further than almost any class of men in the world out of the circle of the conditions needed for the growth and nourishment of Christian morality, of self-sacrifice and brotherly love. Hence the Prelates in Rome have ever been noted for rapacity, arrogance, ambition, sensuality; alternating these indulgences, on occasion, as at the present moment, with vindictiveness and cruelty.

Follow the Catholic priests to England, or, better still, to the United States. Here, without losing the vices inherent in such a theocracy, they become morally as well as intellectually invigorated in the light kindled by Protestantism, to the which they are so unwillingly exposed. They do their best to put out this hated light, feeling that they can never be at home in it, that in the end it must be fatal to them. In Protestant countries priests of Rome always cut somewhat the figure of owls by day.

What intellectual force it has, Catholicism owes to Protestantism. By Protestantism I do not here mean merely Calvinism, or Anglicanism, or Lutheranism, or any other sectarian *ism*, but the imperishable spirit of mental freedom which has in all ages burst up through the crust of ecclesiastical usurpation—the perennial protest of the soul against spiritual authority—the continuous assertion of the rights of conscience. This spirit is the moral life of humanity. The Romish Church, striving ever to crush it, has found in this strife a permanent stimulant to intellectual exertion. In the midst of Protestant churches themselves, this same spirit, struggling ever for absolute liberty, rises up from a deeper deep, protesting against priestly dominion, however tempered. Its sublimest manifestation was against Catholicism through the great Luther, under whose mighty blows the Papacy staggered. In the throes of its despair it gave birth to Jesuitism, which is the offspring of the collision between light and darkness, and which gives evidence in its nature of its monstrous parentage, exhibiting the cold glitter which intellectual light makes on a ground of moral gloom. Jesuitism is henceforth the indispensable armor of Popery.

With the advancement of culture the clerical is overtopped by the literary and scientific classes. A vivifying book rarely comes now-a-days from the clergy, Protestant or Catholic. Creeds are not the nurseries of originality. Original minds on their side are prone to interrogate creeds with very little reverence ; and a heart of deep sympathies solves all theological questions in the flame of its love and justice.

On the other hand, priests, while arrogating to themselves a spiritual superiority, reflect the moral condition of the population around them. Like man, like master. Thus the priest of Mexico fights cocks, and the Cardinal in Rome, and the Anglican Bishop in London play whist. The successors of St. John and St. Peter fighting cocks and playing whist, while Christendom is agasp for want of a vivifying faith ! In all things how effects and causes interplay one upon the other.

Some conclusions :

That a man should never give permanent or irresponsible power over himself to any other man.

That as men are wisely wary of trusting their purses or their persons to others' keeping, much more should they refuse to trust their souls.

That to do so, is to abdicate one's manhood.

That Nature designs the mind to be developed, not moulded.

That irresponsible rulers, priestly or princely, must in the main be knaves; for irresponsibility indurates the conscience.

That force is the law of evil, that is, no law, but like all evil, a breach of law.

Let us return for a moment to Switzerland, whence we have been floated away on this current of thoughts, which are, however, pertinent to her condition; for, republic as she is these five hundred years, she too has had her princes and her priests.

CHAPTER VI.

SWISS REPUBLIC—BADEN-BADEN—THE NUN—PEACE-CONGRESS IN FRANKFORT.

For the most part in Switzerland, political power was from the first absorbed and retained by a few families. In the greater number of Cantons a majority of the inhabitants had no voice in public affairs. Those in which the whole people participated did not contain one tenth of the entire population. Switzerland, strange as this may sound, has learned democracy from France. Until the French revolutions, especially those of –30 and –48, what between the predominance of aristocratic families or of Roman priests, Switzerland was as little progressive as any of her neighbors. She was a Republic with aristocratic institutions—a Republic of the bastard Venetian species. But the democratic element was there and recognized, only not developed. Thence, the popular impulse, communicated by France to Europe, if not caught up with more alacrity by the Swiss than by the Germans, found in them a mould fitted to give it at once practical shape. In the coming conflict between Democracy and Despotism, Switzerland is destined probably to play a part worthy of her origin.

After having been a short time in Switzerland, to be out of it is like resting after work. For the mind that has been weeks on the stretch, heaved up into mountains and furrowed with gorges, the subsiding back to its normal level is a repose. Joy as it was to get into Switzerland, to get out again brought its pleasure. So it ever is with healthy enjoyments; they end naturally, leaving the spirit refreshed for the soberer tenor of its way.

—— From Basle steam hurried us in a few hours to Baden-Baden, whose crowd of motley visitors was waging, as at most "fashionable watering-places," an hourly battle with ennui. By successive assaults of dressing, driving, dining, dancing, gossipping, gambling, strolling, they manage to keep Time under; so that even the professional idler, whose sprightliest companion is his cigar, finds that he can beat "the enemy" day after day, without the trouble of a thought to help him. Then, a Congress of plotters against freedom would hardly have assembled more Kings, and Queens, and princes, the very presence of whom, in such abundance, so magnetized to most of the company the common air, that simple breathing was a continuous intoxication, enough of itself to make life delicious. It would be unjust not to particularize, as the chief attraction of Baden-Baden, its green, varied valleys, and the wooded hills that make them. By help of these, a few choice friends and books, with the privilege—which need not be despised—of cutting at will into the above mentioned artificial stores, a summer might be spent in Baden-Baden in a way that would make one desire to repeat it.

—— From midst the town flights of steps led me, on a Sunday morning, up a steep height, about two hundred feet, to the palace of the Grand Duke. Begilded and bedamasked rooms, empty of paintings or sculpture, were all that there was to see, so I soon passed from the palace to the terrace in front of it.

A landscape looks best on Sunday. With the repose of man Nature sympathizes, and in the inward stillness, imparted unconsciously to every spirit by the general calm, outward beauty is more faithfully imaged.

From the landscape my mind was soon withdrawn, to an object beneath me. Glancing over the terrace-railing almost into the chimneys of the houses below, my eye fell on a female figure in black, pacing round a small garden enclosed by high walls. From the privileged spot where I stood, the walls were no defence, at least against masculine vision. The garden was that of a convent, and the figure walking in it was a nun, upon whose privacy I was thus involuntarily intruding. Never once raising her eyes from her book, she walked round and round the enclosure in the Sabbath stillness. But what to her was this weekly rest? She is herself an incessant sabbath, her existence is a continuous stillness. She has set herself apart from her fellows; she would no more know their work-day doings; she is a voluntary somnambulist, sleeping while awake; she walks on the earth a flesh-and-blood phantom. What a fountain of life and love is there dried up! To cease to be a woman! The warm currents that gush from a woman's heart, all turned back upon their source! What an agony!—And yet, could my eyes, that follow the quiet nun in her circumscribed walk, see through her prison into the street behind it, there they might, perchance at this very moment, fall on a sister going freely whither she listeth, and yet, enclosed within a circle more circumscribed a thousand fold than any that stones can build,—the circle built by public reprobation. Not with downcast lids doth she walk, but with a bold stare that would out-look the scorn she awaits. No Sabbath stillness is for her,—her life is a continuous orgie. No cold phantom is she,—she has smothered her soul in its flesh. Not arrested and stagnant are the currents of her woman's heart,—infected at their spring, they flow foul and fast. Not apart has she set herself from her fellows,—she is thrust out from among them. Her mother knows her no more, nor her father, nor her brother, nor her sister. In exchange for the joys of daughter, wife, mother, woman, she has shame and lust. Great God! What a tragedy she is. To her agony all that the poor nun has suffered is beatitude.—Follow now, in your thought, the two back to their childhood, their sweet chirping innocence. Two dewy buds are they, exhaling from their folded hearts a richer perfume with each maturing month,—two beaming cherubs, that have left their wings behind them, eager to bless and to be blest, and with power to replume themselves from the joys and bounties of an earthly life. In a few short years what a distortion! The one is a withered, fruitless, branchless stem; the other, an unsexed monster, whose touch is poisonous. Can such things be, and men still smile and make merry? To many of its members, society is a Saturn that eats his children—a fiend, that scourges men out of their humanity, and then mocks at their fall.

A nun, like a suicide, is a reproach to Christianity: a harlot is a judgment on civilization.

—In the last days of August, we found ourselves again in Frankfort, at the heels of the Peace-Congress.

Arms can't free a people; ideas only can do that. But at certain stages of the liberating work of ideas, arms have to clear the track for their further march. Otherwise they would be first stopt, and then stifled by gross obstructions. Arms may thus be the instruments of ideas,—impure instruments, but the best, on occasions, that an impure world affords. Threatened with drowning, would you be nice in the means of extrication? Freedom has always used arms; without them she would have been crushed. If honest men should all turn members of the non-resistance society, the rogues would soon have the upper hand.

What can a Peace-Congress do against wolves? Put your preachings into practice in face of a bear. Without compunction or a moment's theoretical cogitation, the meekest zealot of you all, would meet Bruin's hug with the thrust of a bowie-knife. There may be a time when even a bowie-knife can do good service. But a bear is a beast forever inaccessible to thought, which is the parent of freedom and peace. What if you were set upon by a foot-pad, who first wounds you with a pistol-shot, and then rushes forward to rob you, or to finish you with a poignard?

Could you keep your finger off a trigger, or, if you had none, help cursing your stars that you were unarmed. There is but one way of dealing with a murderous assailant. "He who slays with the sword, he shall perish by the sword." The text clearly applies to him, and not to you. Upon him you have fulfilled it, and there an end.

The two millions of soldiers that garrison the continent of Europe, are but legalized foot-pads. They hold bayonets to the throats of the nations, while kings and popes, and their minions, rob their souls and their pockets, and their lives. It is brute force, compelling the mind in its lowest as well as its highest needs, crippling it in all its means. Freedom of speaking, of printing, of meeting, of going and coming, of buying, of selling, of associating,—all are curtailed, hampered, or suppressed. Every right of manhood is maimed or crushed. Against such violence what defence is there? Incalculably more effective arms than pistols, even against pistols themselves, are thoughts—when you can use them. And at this moment, in the face of artillery and the hangman, they are used with an efficiency that startles the gods of gunpowder.

Were the conflict confined to civilized Europe, it might be brought to an end without bloodshed. Vienna and Berlin, and even bemitred Rome would soon capitulate to the fiery assaults of all-conquering thought. But semi-barbarous Russia, who fears freedom and proscribes ideas, puts herself at the head of the brute cause, and gives it her million of muskets. Here is a bear that, under pretence of love for order, would hug freedom to death. And shall Freedom, in this strait, not thrust the sword, not pull the trigger?

Let the Peace-Congress address itself to the Emperor of Russia. He is the chief, nay, the only obstacle to peace in Europe. With an unchristian infidelity the Emperor of Russia puts his trust in the despotism of muskets. With his brute force he upholds the regal governments of the Continent, the which, being dead, can only be upheld by brute force. At Paris and Rome, as well as at Vienna and Berlin, Russian policy rules. But for her, Freedom, the nursery of peace, would be already founded on the ruins of Austrian despotism, and her cause be triumphant in Germany. The logical place for the next Peace-Congress is Warsaw.

The Despots have divined, that peace can only be the fruit of freedom. Thence they regard the Peace-Congress as a Freedom-Congress. It is a Freedom-Congress. But can it devise how, in the actual array of hostilities, freedom can triumph without a temporary alliance with gunpowder? Most of its members are, I suspect, of one mind with three American delegates whom I had the pleasure of meeting in Switzerland on their way to Frankfort, whose tongues warmed at the talk of a universal armed uprising of the Peoples against the tyrants that degrade and despoil them.

CHAPTER VII.

STAGE-COACH AND CAR—CONSERVATISM—GERMAN BURGHER AND POSTILION—PRIMARY EDUCATION IN GERMANY.

Among agreeable contrasts cannot be classed that between a steam-driven car and a German stage-coach. On the railroad from Frankfort to Cassel, there was, in 1850, between Friedberg and Giessen, a chasm which we were three hours in getting over by coach. What a good thing is a McAdam road! It deserves the point of admiration. Wherewith then shall we point the sentence that tells of the railroad? To pass from the one to the other is like poverty after affluence, like a good whistler after Jenny Lind, like beer after Burgundy. How we grapple to us what we once get possession of. Who would give up the railroad or the newspaper? Ask the freshman to go back to the school-room. A progress takes hold of us like the growing fibre of our frame: it enfolds our life. To go back, is against nature. Our lot is, to go forward.

Let Conservatives bethink them. Our moral life is as sluggish as the "Royal Mail." Only twenty years ago the mail's ten miles an hour was very fast. 'Twas the most that turnpike and coach could do. Who then talked of twenty miles the hour, not to speak of fifty, was a dangerous innovator or an impractical Utopian. The ten miles is the most can be got out of the old Church and the old State. We want a new Church, as different from the old one as iron and steam are from horse-flesh and granite. Who dare say "Halt," to the moral man? Why should I doubt that we may have a belief so inspiring, that our social condition shall, like locomotive speed, rise from ten to fifty. Are we only mechanical? Can we reform roads and not institutions? Are no more discoveries to be made in the upper sphere? Have we read to the end of the book of life, that we turn back the leaves to the first chapters again? In the presence of miraculous man, and the mighty Providence above him, who dare define his possibilities? Ye think yourselves believers, and ye believe only in the dead and the dying. The Barbarian believes naught but tradition and what he sees. Ye bandage your vision with his limitations: ye forego the right of reason, which bids ye look before as well as after. Talk to the Barbarian of the railroad and the electric telegraph; he will laugh at you, if he does not frown. Talk we to you of methods whereby evil shall be exorcised and good made to prevail like sunshine, of harmonies that shall convert human labor into a life-long joy, of conditions that shall fulfil your daily prayer, "thy kingdom come, thy will be done on earth as it is in heaven,"—ye laugh or frown. Ye civilized barbarians, ye believing skeptics, upon ye be this triple malediction; ye shall sail without the compass, travel without steam, and read never a printed page.

—By my side on the top of the coach, was an average sample of a German Burgher,—stout and kindly, intelligent and accessible. It did me good to hear him curse all kings, particularly his own of Prussia. Not that as a democrat I need to be fortified in my political creed by this verbal pulling down of monarchies; or, that as a man I take delight in hearing a fellow-man, even a king, abused. It was as evidence,—such as I have had much of in the past few weeks,—of the emancipation of German feeling from the thraldom of regal prestige, that I listened with pleasure to my neighbor's king-cursing fluency. No "divinity doth hedge a king" any more in Germany. In the Frankfort

Assembly, two years ago, an orator said bitingly of his countrymen, " A German without a prince, is like a dog without a master." He could not and would not have said it, if it had not already begun to cease to be true. In these two years the Germans have not made progress simply, they have made a leap. They have, in opinions and convictions, leapt clean out of princedom. One is astonished to hear of and to witness the so rapid and general conversion to democracy. Principles of political liberty and resolves to put them into act, are widely spread and deeply rooted. Among this thoughtful, reading people, the ground was well prepared, and the princes by their perfidy are doing almost better for the growing crop, than could have done those who are to reap. There will be a plentiful harvest; if it be gathered in blood, the blood be on the heads of the traitors who, having been again trusted, would again rule with the old tyrannies. In two years what a revulsion! After the popular victory in 1848, how forgiving, hopeful, magnanimous, trustful, was the whole German race: in 1850, how full of wrath, bitterness, menace. There will be no forgiveness of the past the next time.

In the postilion, who from the back of the near wheel-horse conducted our cumbrous vehicle, I had a sample of a German proletarian. Proletarian means a producer of men. The day-laborers of Europe are esteemed, first as workers, who can be bought at about twenty-five cents a day, to do all agricultural and manufacturing work; and secondly, as breeders, whose function is to keep full the supply of workers. Hence this appellation, which denotes that the masses here are valued as muscle-endowed animals, not as soul-endowed men. Our postilion had been twenty-six years on the road, passing over these same few leagues almost daily; and yet, of the small neighboring towns or villages, so near that the spires and highest buildings were visible, he knew the name of scarcely one. His countryman by my side, poured upon him from our elevation, volleys of bitter ridicule.

The postilion was annoyed, not at being found ignorant, but that he was expected to know such things. In his *naïveté* there was wisdom, as there so often is. His feeling was an unconscious protestation, that personally he was blameless for his ignorance. They are the blamable, who, under pretext of governing, convert a man into a carriage-conducting machine.

Much praise has been bestowed on the schools, and on the universality of primary instruction in Germany. For the comparative excellence of methods and the breadth of their application, let the praise stand. Good schooling is never a bad thing. Nevertheless, when for twelve hours out of the twenty-four, men are turned into beasts of burden, and can then barely earn the coarsest food and raiment, how much does schooling profit them? Many of the German peasants are found in mature life, to have forgotten how to read and write. What time or occasion have they to use these high instruments? To men so belabored, so disfranchised, schooling is almost a mockery. This postilion can read and write. Had he been never taught a letter, but been allowed a voice in naming the mayor of his village, and the parson of his church, I warrant he would have known the names of every hamlet we passed; and this in itself, barren knowledge, would have been the attendant and sign of a productive knowledge of men and things, denoting that his understanding had been cultivated by animating contacts, and his heart enlarged by sympathies beyond the petty routine of the postilion's duties. Let him vote for his burgomaster, his pastor, and his tax-imposer, and no fear but he will take care that his children be provided with the humanizing media of intercourse, reading, writing, and arithmetic; and no fear either that they will forget them from want of practice. The mere introduction of the penny-post in England, led tens of thousands of poor people to learn to read and write, just to avail themselves of the facility thus opened of communicating with their distant relatives. Open to the laborer the facility and necessity of communicating with his neighbors and fellow-men,—his political relatives,—on their common interests and rights; give him as man the practical education acquired by a manly share in public affairs, and he will be sure to provide,—whether by public or private means,—for the school-instruction of the boy. But this elevation of the proletarian is the reverse of what European governments desire.

CHAPTER VIII.

MARBURG—MONUMENT—RAILROAD TO CASSEL—CASSEL TO DRESDEN.

To the traveller on this route, who travels to see, I recommend half a day at Marburg. A prettier site for a small inland town, he will seldom meet with. It stands on the sides of a hill that projects like a sudden promontory into the valley of the Lahn, and whose summit is crowned with the old castle of the Landgraves of Hesse, round which the town gradually built itself in the middle ages. At the outer base of the promontory is the church, pure and simple Gothic, six hundred years old, with double towers, remarkable for its symmetry. The station is a quarter of a mile distant from the town. As you sweep up to it on the curve of the railroad, the castle on the top of the hill, the old town on its sides, the graceful church at its foot, with a valley running back from its northern slope, make a picture so captivating, that you rejoice to learn that this is Marburg, where you are to stop.

On our way up to the castle, we passed the houses wherein had lodged Luther and Zwingli, when they met here to discuss transubstantiation. They of course parted without agreeing. To settle a theological question is as easy as to pin a ghost to the wall: they are both so purely within the province of the imagination. In the castle is a chapel, in which Luther preached. I mounted into the plain oaken pulpit, whence the thunderer had launched his church-rending lightnings.

The town, partly in shadow, clustered round the protecting castle, the twin, tapering spires, and the soft valley of the Lahn, seen up and down, combine to give a view from the terrace which, in the afternoon especially, is enchanting. As we gazed, a train from Cassel came down the valley. After rushing noisily past in front of us, it shot away in silence to the south, under its white canopy of mist, like a cloud before a hurricane.

—— To "take mine ease in mine inn," the inn must be good. The inn is the traveller's home, and he can't feel at home in it unless it be cleanly and kindly. Mine host and hostess are the wayfarer's father and mother. When he alights they receive him with welcome, good cheer, and a clean bed. These he will find at the "Golden Knight" (zum Goldnen Ritter), in Marburg. Mine host was a good specimen of the German Boniface of a small town—portly, thriving, communicative, familiar but respectful, a good judge of meat and drink, and sharing fairly with his guests the fruits of his judgment. Twice a year he goes to the Rhine to replenish his cellar. While there he keeps his palate susceptible by abstinence, and surrenders himself to the gustative joy which the Rhine offers to the discriminating connoisseur, not until after he has made his purchases. He warmed towards me as he perceived that I drank in with relish his discourse about the localities where *Liebfrauenmilch*, *Oppenheimer*, *Niersteiner* ripen. As compliment to his publican qualities, and as index of his thrift, he owns a garden on the skirt of the town. His landlordship were incomplete without these few acres within an easy walk of his door, where he rears fruit and esculents, and has a daily pastime for his latter years. I am bound to mention, for the truthfulness of my sketch, that at parting the next afternoon, he played me a very unfatherly trick, having—after we had paid his bill and set out on foot to the station—manifested a hard-hearted indifference whether our luggage arrived in time or not. Had I met him within the ten minutes of excruciating suspense caused by his coldness, I should have had difficulty in refraining from paying his unparental insensibility with very unfilial phrases.

After exploring the pretty valley that runs back and brings a tributary brook of most limpid water to the Lahn, we ascended a hill across it directly opposite to the town, wishing to get a view from this point, and attracted too by a monument on the summit of the hill. The view is a reward for the ascent to any one who does not find in the walk itself its own reward; and the monument I would not have missed seeing had the road to it been rugged and steep.

I defy all the millions of guessers in the United States to divine why this monument was erected. No American imagination could in such a search come near enough to have even "warm" cried to it, as in the game of Hunt the Slipper. After looking round at the panoramic landscape, I turned towards the monument, an obelisk twelve or fourteen feet high, built of freestone. When I had read the inscription, I read it over again. Yes, there could be no mis-reading; the words were plain, well-cut German. I am counting perhaps much too largely upon my character for veracity, in hoping that it will be able to withstand the shock of the reader's incredulity, when I tell him that their purport was as follows. A princess of Hesse-Cassel had one fine day walked up to this spot, and enjoyed the views thence. To commemorate this fact this monument of stone was built by some grateful inhabitants of Marburg. And these good Germans would at times take airs over us on account of African slavery! I must in justice add that it is a monument of the past, having been raised about thirty years ago.

—— At every station of the road to Cassel on Sunday afternoon, crowds of peasants were assembled to see the steam-wonder. At the snorting monster, fire-souled, and wheel-pawed, they stared as the aboriginal Americans did at the vessels of Columbus. But not like them with wild wonderment and a dim presentient fear. The white civilizee is within reach of the beneficence of machinery; for the yellow savage it is an unsparing destroyer, which mows him down the faster in proportion as itself is the stronger. At the flying "locomotive," whose wings, laden with a hundred men, outfly the eagle, the sun-browned sons and daughters of labor gazed with an intelligent admiration, as half conscious that it is a harbinger of better days.—For the emancipation of man all powers must co-work; the intellect with its logic and its inventions, the soul with its expansive wants, nature with the revelations which she so gladly makes to penetrative genius. Industry must join hands with Christianity, Science with Sentiment, Intelligence with Faith. The momentum of humanity must have been already incalculably accelerated by the unfolding of its capacities, ere it can swing itself into a wider orbit. This momentum it now has; and as the train, burthened with its scores of tons, swept with fabulous speed past turretted burgs and stately castles in ruin, it was a symbol of the present eager movement among the foremost nations of Christendom, striding forward with new energy and new hope, leaving behind the old walls and towers of defence, and careering into a sphere of untrammelled freedom and unvexed enjoyment.

—— At Cassel, the population was all out of doors, in the great streets and in the public walks, as is the continental custom of a Sunday afternoon, the peasantry from the neighborhood flocking in to diversify and thicken the crowd. Puppets, mountebanks, and monkeys were entertaining full-grown men and women. The pleasure of the lower classes in these childish spectacles, is reflected in the upper, who delight to see them enjoy such coarse emptinesses, it being a sign that they are themselves empty and childish, and therefore governable. To be easily governed is, in the eyes of governors, the highest virtue of a people. I am happy to bear witness that this virtue is here growing weaker and weaker. A manly consciousness is awakened in the laborious masses. Thence the multiplication of soldiers, who are the constables of tyrants. On these musket-shouldering drones, the people now scowl with feelings anything but childlike.

Between Cassel and Dresden lie five or six degrees of longitude, and the territories of half a dozen sovereign states. This space, dotted with towns of historic name, has on the map a formidable look, Cassel lying in the west, and Dresden in the east of Germany. But the wishing-cap of Gothic mythology finds its realization in a railroad ticket. Wish yourself three hundred miles off, and by having in your pocket a printed slip of paper, your wish is in a twinkling fulfilled, even in Germany, where the fiery "Locomotive" has to curb his impatience, and adapt his flight somewhat to the proverbial Teutonic slowness.

CHAPTER IX.

A DAY IN DRESDEN.

Dresden, the capital of Saxony, contains 90,000 inhabitants; its collections of works of art have gained for it the title of "the German Florence;" its two unequal parts are united by a broad substantial stone bridge over the Elbe, "built with money raised by the sale of dispensations from the Pope for eating butter and eggs during Lent," &c. &c. The &cs. covering twenty closely printed pages, the reader, curious in such details, will find in "Murray's Hand-Book for Northern Germany." Here he will have only the sketch of a day in Dresden, from notes, taken down on the spot, of such "Scenes and Thoughts" as presented themselves successively to the writer, from early morning till bed-time, on Monday, the 9th of September, 1850.

Through a window of No. 16, a spacious chamber on the second floor of the Hotel, *Stadt Rom*, I look, while dressing, into the square of the *Neu-Markt*, yet in shadow, for it is half-past six o'clock. Carts, and women bearing on their backs heavily laden baskets, are coming slowly in from the country. Opposite, across the square, is the great Picture-Gallery; at the right, the "Church of our Lady," with its stone dome, large and lofty, illuminated by the rising sun.

—— Before seven, out in the cool morning. Fires are already lighted, in people's mouths. We have just past a cart drawn by a woman and dog, pulling sociably in harness together, and at every few steps, we come upon women stooping as they walk, under burthens on their backs. Striking into a street raked by the sun,—for the air is chilly,—we soon issue upon the *Wills-druffer* Place, set off by a fountain in form of an elaborate, feathery, Gothic pinnacle; and thence onward to the *Zwinger*, an extensive showy edifice, where are the Historical and other Museums, partly destroyed during the late civil conflicts. The sides of the building enclose a square, laid out in walks and shrubbery. Before entering, let us read the printed notice at the gate-way:—"These grounds are recommended to the protection of the public." A greeting like this, wins at a stroke the affection of the stranger. Such gentle fraternal words, tell of refinement and mutual trust. They made sacred to us every blade and leaf within the enclosure. We walked back to the inn with the sensation that one has, after receiving welcome unexpected news.

The carts in the New Market-place have emptied their loads, which are now piled up breast high on one side of the square, pile next to pile of huge loaves of rye bread, baked in the neighboring villages.

Waiting for breakfast in the public room of the *Stadt Rom*, from a seat by the corner window, I have a level view of the whole square, and a close one of the current of passers in and out of it, through a street that runs by one side of the hotel. People have not a brisk auroral air; they look relaxed instead of braced. They don't go at the day vigorously. This early aspect of awakened Dresden, is of a town that takes its leisure. After breakfast, I sauntered across to the sunny corner of the square, towards the church, where the market-women with their baskets of vegetables are chatting and chaffering. Their heads are without covering. If upon the living brain the sun could breed thought, as upon the dead he breeds maggots, what vaulted brows would crown the faces of European peasânts, what Moses-like coruscations would shoot from their parturient foreheads. But then they would cease to be peasants, to be the drudge-horses and patient oxen that they are. The sun breeds only brownness and dryness, which embellish not the feminine physiognomy. The market-women, however, look ruddy and cheerful, and show well, as country people always do, by the side of the townfolk.

—— At nine, by appointment, with other sight-seers, to the Green Vault (*das Grüne Gewölbe*),—a regal curiosity-shop, stocked with Mosaics, jewels, trinkets, miniature-carvings in wood, ivory, and precious metals, and other costly rarities. Here and there is a bit having the unworn stamp of beauty ; but the most of them are not works of Art ; that is, works embodying thought, sentiment, or vivid corporeal reality in beautiful forms. They are skilful handiwork, with little head or heart-work ; the toilsome shapings of uninspired fancy ; the lifeless leavings of Art, elaborate nothings ; fruits of the patronizings of tasteless Princes. The most precious jewels were absent, having been removed for safe-keeping to the Fortress of Königstein. They showed us one unique natural product,—a crystal globe twenty-two inches in circumference, a solid transparence, a flawless mineral purity, purged by subterranean fires.

The Historical Museum is an abstract, written in daggers and breastplates, of the history of war during the latter half of what are called the middle ages. These coats of mail are contemplated with a certain favor if one will regard them as life-preservers during the stormy period of chivalry. After all, these old-time brawlers and spoilers took devilish good care of their skins. Just before quitting the Museum we came unexpectedly upon arms of a totally different and immensely more effective kind, the pen of Goethe and the modelling-stick of Thorwaldsen. These modest, tiny weapons, what conquests have they not made! They lay in their little case a mordant irony on the performances of the Duke Georges and Prince Henrys, whose effigies on horseback, armed cap-à-pié, we had just seen, and whose exploits, only heard of through the mouth of the droning cicerone, we had already forgotten. It is a humane surprise prepared for the visitor, thus to quicken his spirit with these modern holy relics, after it has been wearied with such a flat reiteration of profane antiquities.

—— We have time before dinner to look upon some of the splendors in the Collection of Pictures, one of the richest in Europe. Passing with hasty glances through the broad galleries, hung by the procreant hand of genius, we soon found ourselves at their centre, before the masterpiece of masterpieces, the *Madonna di Sto. Sisto* of Raphael. When, after gazing at it often, you happen to be in the congenial receptive mood, which a work of art demands, in order to be appreciated, the wonderful perfections of this picture reveal themselves. Those two heads, the Mother and Child! In the Madonna is the plenitude of womanly life and beauty; grace united with power, strength with sweetness. What a grand contour of head, yet soft and feminine; calm, earnest, with a deep look of unspeakable beatitude. The whole and the individual features, regular as Greeks could have made them, and yet without coldness or limitation, but warm as happiest maternity and of infinite suggestiveness.—The Child has a wise, almost wizard look. But for the earnestness and mystic depth in the eyes, one might think it the head of an urchin who would prove hard to manage,—and in truth the man Jesus was unmanageable, a protestor and reformer, a rebel against the priestcraft of his time. The big eyes look like loop-holes through which the Past is peering thoughtfully and sadly into the Future. The hair is wild and unkempt. The head and face are not regular, but running over with beauty; infantile and beyond childhood; shining with an inward light, that ennobles the features with the glow of human intellect and sympathy. With the instinct of genius, Raphael has made the head large, but the size is absorbed by the light of the expression.—The two up-gazing Cherubs at the base,—the types of love and joy, the focusses of infinite rapture, marvellous little winged heads,—are in power and beauty entirely subordinated to the unwinged Jesus.—This is a picture that Fame has never caught up with.

Ere we quit the Gallery let us pause for a moment before another of its chief treasures,—Neptune stilling the Tempest, by Rubens. At the command of Neptune, standing in a shell borne on the waves by sea-horses with heads and necks above water, and followed by sea-nymphs, the angry winds with black wings are reluctantly retiring. What breadth and power of conception, expression and coloring. One is nerved by looking at this picture. Those three prancing heads are a great creation. Rubens has here brought to view the original types of the horse species, the progenitors of the whole equine race, such fire is there and inexhaustible strength, such a nervous dilation in those heads, darting lightnings from eye and nostril.

—— At one,—a wholesome hour,—we sat down with a score of fellow-diners to the public dinner in the hotel. The dishes, served successively, were soup, fish, mutton-chops with red cabbage, roast veal, rice pudding—a modest repast which cost forty cents in money and one hour and a quarter in time.

—— The human capacity of adaptation is nowhere more forcibly exhibited than in the acquired callousness to the suffering which, in Europe especially, assaults the compassion at every turn, and which, but for this pliancy to circumstances, would keep the spirits forever low and banish smiles from the countenance of man. But there are spectacles to which no use of custom can so harden us but that the heart will always sadden in their presence. In going up to our chamber after dinner we had one of these,—a woman bearing on her back such a load of wood, that as she slowly set foot before foot in the ascent, so bent was she under the weight that her face and hands almost touched the step above, her burthen thus converting her corporeally, as it tends to do spiritually, into a down-looking quadruped. One hurries by such sights, that the pang they give may be quickly quenched in the sea of busy movement about us; but against them, and even against those to which we are outwardly hardened, men enter more and more frequently and more and more deeply an inward protest as they pass. A fact full of hope is the accumulating protestation against cruelty and wrong. This ceaseless heart-cry is a prophecy. Feeling precedes conviction, conviction precedes action. The one predicts the other. A present ideal of healthy minds is the promise of a future reality. They whose convictions outrun their practice, whose aspirations are purer than their deeds, who know the littlenesses of our dislocated existence for what they are, let them cherish uplifting thoughts; these are not barren dreams, they are the roots of a more generous life.

Who is this that greets us at the landing with an humble smile from her arch face? Her face is more than arch, it is pretty besides, and would be more than pretty, were the soul that lights it itself fully lighted. Her brown hair is carried back in that easiest simple manner called Grecian. Her head turns gracefully on a fair round neck; and her shoulders, bust, waist, and whole figure are in harmony with her head. Her arm, bare and white, would fix the eye of Greenough or of Powers in admiration, while on his organ of form he took its impress for ideal uses. Were you to meet her in a cottage, you would think the cottage blest by her sweetness,—in a drawing-room of jewelled beauties, she would seem to be born for this elegant rivalry,—in a Palace, you might forget the Princess in the woman. Poor Saxon Girl, whose mien doth beget for thee such divers perfections upon the imagination of a passing stranger, lower than the most modest of these conditions is thy lot. Not for thee is even the cottage, with the breadth of earth and sky to compensate for its cabined uncultured existence. Perhaps from its rustic hearth thou wast lured by the glare of the city, towards which,—impelled by the deep need of human communion,—so many of thy sisters rush to burn their ignorant wings in its fire, and to drag ever after their blackened bodies towards an obscure grave. Thee Nature destined for a higher sphere. Where the texture is, the sculptor's creative hand fashions the Goddess from the raw block: thou hast the texture wherewith the plastic power of favoring circumstances could have fashioned a household Goddess, an honored accomplished woman. But Fortune, to whose caprices so many are committed in this blind-folded world, not joining hands with Nature, thou wast disorbed, and now dost perform,—and that with the cheerfulness of a happy temperament,—the low daily routine allotted to the chambermaid of an inn.

How few people are in their right places. And worse still; were there to be a thorough shuffling, a general change and interchange of conditions and positions, forward and backward and sideways and upward and downward, still we should not get into them. The right places are not there.

—— Dresden has attractive environs. But the weather is just now so unseasonably cold, that an open carriage is rather a penance than a pleasure. We shall content ourselves this afternoon with an intramural stroll. The town has an air of old-fashioned elegance. There is a courtly quiet in the streets. Business and traffic are secondary. Many of the people that you meet seem to have nothing to do, and those who bear on them some badge of business are going about it so leisurely, that most of them, one would think, will be overtaken by to-morrow ere they get through. The absence of commercial bustle is an agreeable characteristic of Dresden.

At six we walked to the large, commodious theatre lately erected near the river. The piece was an opera, a good one, *The Water-carrier.* About the time that the curtain of the opera in London and Paris rises, that of Dresden falls. At half-past eight we were back to the hotel, taking a late tea, while our neighbors, male and female, at the public table were busy with the early German supper of meat, bread, cheese, and salad, of which last, especially, the Germans, who have an enviable gift of copious feeding, consume a huge quantity.

—— It is past nine. Although the opera is over, the Dresden day is not yet closed. If the reader will go along with me, I will bring him where he will witness what, if he has not been in Germany, he never has witnessed. In a few minutes we are on the *Brühl* Terrace, which forms a delightful walk within the town, along the river and high above it. Here is a *café:* we pay a few coppers at the door, and enter a hall capable of holding three hundred people: it is now quite full. At the opposite end, a large band of good performers is executing excellent music. The company, half females, are seated at numerous tables of different sizes, supplied with coffee, tea, beer, wine, and some with eatables. This kind of cheap, good, sociable, conversational concert, is characteristic of Germany. One feature caps its Germanism: nearly all the men are smoking. One hundred of them simultaneously puffing out smoke generated in their mouths by their lungs, which act as bellows on ignited tobacco, in a closed hall neither large nor lofty, where, intermingled with the smoke-producers, are one hundred and fifty of the softer (I cannot here say sweeter) sex, witnesses of the production, and absorbents of the product. The throng of people sit for hours in the compound rankness of this unventilated hall, with an insensibility to bad air that verified with clenching emphasis, how custom may usurp upon nature. If the lungs and olfactory nerves of delicate women will not protest, their shawls and silks should, against this foul violation of the rights of women. For ourselves, as dutiful sight-seers, we bore the pressure upon the arterial circulation of this deoxygenated nicotenized atmosphere for twenty minutes, and then fled to the terrace. The Germans do not smoke, they are smoked. Tobacco has got the upper hand of them.

By ten we were back to the hotel and No. 16.

CHAPTER X.

WEIMAR—CEMETERY—SCHILLER'S STUDY—GALL AND GOETHE—CRANIUM OF SCHILLER—WEIMAR'S HIGH INHABITANTS.

The next day towards noon we were suddenly beset by a desire to be in Weimar. I like in travelling to give way to an impulse of this kind. In the wilful breaking up of the set sequence of things, there is a remunerative assurance of freedom. You start without the ceremony of giving yourself notice. You go solely because you want to go. In this there is an enlivening breach of routine, a luxury of liberty. You snatch a sunny holiday from amidst the sombre slaveries of this conventional, whip-driven world. After a hurried packing, we provided ourselves with the modern wishing-cap, and alighted by early bed-time at the "Hereditary Prince," in Weimar, having rushed through book-selling Leipzig and book-fed Halle, just as though, instead of being populous, notable towns, they had been only relay houses by the wayside.

—— I walked again in my old paths through the tranquil town of Weimar. 'Tis like arresting, and fixing in hard corporeality, the airy images of a dream, thus to re-behold after twenty-five years, the scenes of careless, laughing youth. The solid recognized forms are as cold and sad-speaking as the sarcophagi of departed friends. One hovers about them with a melancholy self-abandonment. I think I know how a ghost feels who revisits the haunts of his sublunary sojourn. I peered as I went into faces, with a hope of recognition or reciprocated interest; but all were cold, exclusive, introverted, just like the faces of other streets. I passed before Goethe's house. At that door I had once knocked, —with timidity, as having no claim to admittance but that which his fame gave me,—and within I had met, shining with kindliness, that great glittering eye. For what is left of his mortal part I must now seek in the vault.

And thither I bent my steps. He who after the lapse of a quarter of a century revisits the resorts of his youth, must betake him to the graveyard to find the vestiges of his former acquaintance. The cemetery of Weimar, lying just outside the town, has an untrimmed look which suits a cemetery. Flowers and shrubbery and grass are not much curtailed of their natural freedom. This wildness and unclipt exuberance is in harmony with the spot, and gives to it a softer and a quieter aspect. In the centre is a small chapel for funeral services. Through the middle of the floor a large round opening, guarded by a balustrade, communicates with the Grand-ducal vault below, wherein, with those of the sovereign family, lie the bodies of Goethe and Schiller. We descended by the stairway into the vault. It was neither dark nor damp, and was mildly perfumed by burnt incense. Here was naught of the gloom of a charnel-house. 'Twas as though the immortal spirits of the great inmates had purified it of all stains of death. Beside their holy remains we lingered with feelings of cheerful elevation. It was not a place for sadness. The coffins are raised three or four feet from the ground. Those containing the bodies of Goethe and Schiller are side by side, apart from the others. I stood between them, with my hands resting one on either coffin.

The late Grand-Duke of Weimar, Charles Augustus, the friend of Goethe and Schiller, and who is illustrious by that friendship, requested that his body should be placed between the bodies of the two Poets. He had a right to make the request: he was worthy of that exalted place. He was not merely their friend and generous protector; he had a soul that sympathized with theirs. Whether it be, that his successors, animated by a low jealousy, are unwilling to recognize his right to this great privilege, or that they are influenced by a still more ignoble motive, his request has not yet been complied with. The coffin containing his body lies by itself.

—— In the study of Schiller I sat down one morning at his desk, and with ink dipped from an inkstand of Goethe, I took phrenological notes on a cast of Schiller's head. There was a seat and an occupation! But nothing is complete in this loose, fragmentary world. Why was there no mould from the cranium of Schiller's renowned friend? Because men are such laggards behind truth. The momentous, brilliant discovery of the physiology of the brain was promulgated in the beginning of this century, and first in Germany by its great discoverer, Gall. And still, though so easily verified, it remains unacknowledged by scientific men on the continent of Europe. In freer England, and freest America, its truth has been forced upon the scientific in a great measure by the enlightened perseverance of the laity. Goethe, whose sympathy with the spirit and processes of Nature was the source of his wisdom, meeting with Gall, who, in a tour through Germany, was expounding his newly-made discovery, received it at once into his mind, with that large hospitality which he always extended to new-comers from the realms of Nature. Pity that he had not cultivated acquaintanceship into intimacy. His name would have been a passport to this fruitful truth, and thus have hastened by half a century its acceptance among his countrymen. In that case, moreover, his friends and executors, knowing the scientific value of a fac-simile of his noble head, we should have had his by the side of Schiller's, to compare together and contrast the two.

The brain of Schiller, from its large size and general conformation, denotes uncommon energy, great force and warmth of character, and irresistible mental momentum. In his organization there was a rich mingling of powers. What he undertook he went at with a zeal that rallied his whole nature to the service, with a volume of impetus that bore him on with burning velocity, and with a resolution that no obstacle could stay. His undertakings were high, his aspirations noble. Onward, onward, upward, upward! might have been his device. With all this fiery enthusiasm, this impatient activity, he undertook naught rashly. He was at once impetuous and prudent. He was self-confident, but with consciousness of his gifts he united an insatiable thirst for better than he could furnish. His ideal was so exalted it kept him ever learning and expanding. Goethe was often astonished, when they would meet after a not very long separation, to find what progress he had made in the interval. His intellect was under the spur of his poetic expansions fed by his hearty impulses. His mind was kept at red heat. His nature was earnest, and even stern. If there was in him no sportiveness or humor, neither was there any littleness. His love of fame was strong, but he sought to gratify it by lofty labors.

Schiller's intellect was broad and massive, not subtle nor penetrative. Hence, with all his material of sympathy and inborn passion, wherewith he energized and diversified his characters, they lack individuality and compactness. In the most finished there is a certain hollowness. It is not so much, that they are not distinctly enough differenced one from the other, as that each is not tightly knit up into itself, as in Shakspeare and Goethe. Schiller was not the closest, most scrupulous thinker, and thence in creating characters he could not thoroughly interpenetrate the animal and sentimental vitality with the intellectual, which interpenetration must be in order that each personage have his definite, rounded, vivacious existence. Nor is the action in his dramatic structures always bound up in the severest logical chain. Schiller was not a Poet of the highest order; he was not prophetic, not a *vates*. He did not deliver truths, or embody beauty in creations, so much above the standard of his age that they have to wait for a higher culture to be fully valued. His generalizations have not the unfading brilliancy which those truths have that are wrought in the mine of emotion by the intensest action of reason. Between his intellect and his sensibility there was not that perfect accord which makes the offspring of their union at once veracious and ideal, and elastic from the compactness of their constituents. His grasp of intellect was not so strong as was his imaginative swing. When the cast was put into my hands what first struck me was the want of prominence in the upper part of the forehead.

Speaking of his early flight from Wurtemberg, Schiller describes the joy he felt in having thenceforward no other master than the Public. To an ardent young Poet it could not but be a joy, akin to that of moral renovation, to escape from the suffocation of tyranny, to find himself rid of a narrow King and face to face with the broad multitude. But there is a still higher Tribunal,—through which too the Public is in the end more surely and permanently won than by direct appeal to itself,—the tribunal of Truth. To this and this alone the true Artist feels himself amenable. For, the Artist's function is, to purify the sensibility of his fellow-men, to instruct them by awakening a poetic admiration, to chasten their taste. By creations in harmony with the absolute true and beautiful, he develops, and cultivates the latent æsthetic capability of the mass. His part is to be a teacher, not a flatterer or prosaic purveyor. Great Artists are always above their Public. Did Shakspeare suit himself to the common judgment of his day? So little so, that even the shrewdest of his contemporaries discerned not half the meaning and merit of his wonderful creations. He himself,—sublime isolation,—was the only one of his time who knew their transcendent worth. To think, that for more than a century there was in the whole world but one man who entirely enjoyed the Tempest and Lear, who was capable of fully loving Imogen and Juliet, and that man was Shakspeare. What kind of appeal to the general judgment of Charles the Second's generation was Paradise Lost? Wordsworth scorned the Public, who laughed at him, and having survived a half-century his earlier Poems, had the personal enjoyment of a tardy justice, his genius being acknowledged by a more "enlightened Public" than that which first so coldly greeted him, his later contemporaries paying him reverence as a true Priest in the service of Beauty and Truth. He had to make the taste by which he was appreciated. Goethe, mentioning in a letter to Schiller, the limited sale of one of his best Poems, *Hermann and Dorothea,* comforts himself by adding ironically,—"we make money by our bad books." And Schiller himself, who always wrote in pursuit of a refined ideal, says somewhere, that the Artist's mission is to scourge rather than to truckle to the spirit of his age.

It is much for a man to possess several eminent qualities that keep him on a high level. Schiller was upborne by his poetic nature and his love of humanity. He had not the deepest sensibility for truth. Thus, although, under his poetic and generous inspirations, he appreciated and practically fulfilled the Artist's function, his impulse when first freed was towards fame. From the same source,—that is, the absence of arched rotundity in the region of conscientiousness,—I would infer a want of punctuality in engagements, literary and other, and venture to conjecture, that by this failing his friend Goethe was occasionally somewhat put out.

Among the precious relics was the bedstead whereon Schiller slept, and whereon he died at the early age of forty-six. Often at night, he put his feet into a tub of cold water, placed under his writing-table, in order thereby to keep himself awake. He worked his brain to the uttermost, and wore himself out with the noblest labor. It were easy to figure him seated at his desk, with "visionary eye" and furrowed brow, intently elaborating thoughts which his pen hurriedly seized, when a knock, drawing from him an unwilling "Herein," he would lift his eyes with a look of almost sternness, for the unwelcome interrupter; and then suddenly his countenance would relax and beam, as the tall figure of Goethe advanced through the opening door, and rising with an eager motion, he would greet his friend with cordial words and hand-grasp. And the fever of his mind would subside. The calm power of the self-possessing Goethe would soothe him without lowering his tone; and when, after Goethe's departure, he set himself again to his work, it would be with the refreshed feeling of one who, towards the close of a midsummer's day, has just bathed in the shady nook of a deep, tranquil stream.

On one side of the desk is a sliding chess-board, to be drawn out when wanted. Here, the guardian of the house declared, Goethe and Schiller sometimes played. This I refused to credit, and put it down as a false tradition. Games,—even those involving bodily exercise,—are the resource of the vacant; and I would not believe that two such full-brained men, whose interviews were to them both enlivening thought-breeders, would ever dedicate their tête-à-tête meetings to this solemn frivolity, this ingenious emptiness, this silent, sapless pastime. Still, against the circumstantial conclusions of reason, there was the sliding chess-board.

——Owing to some misunderstanding between Goethe's heirs and executors, his house is only opened one day in the week, and even then his study is not shown. On entering the drawing-room, I perceived that there had been crowded into it sets of porcelain, piles of prints, vases, and other articles such as a man of Goethe's celebrity and tastes would, in a long life, collect by purchase or gift. The room looked like a crammed curiosity-shop. Without exchanging a word with a person who was there to serve as expounder, I turned back, and with feelings of disgust instead of satisfaction, left the house.

I contented myself with the outside of the abodes of Herder and Wieland.

——After I had studied the cast from Schiller's cranium, and had thoughtfully wrought out a correspondence between it and his mental endowments as exhibited in his life and writings, fitting the cast to the character, and the character to the cast, as is the pleasant way with phrenologists, I learnt from a gifted physician in Weimar, that there was a slight—a very slight—doubt as to whether the cranium from which the cast had been taken, was that of Schiller. When, many years after his death, the bones of Schiller were dug up, to be removed to the Grand-ducal vault, it was found, that his body had been buried so near to two others, that the sexton was not absolutely certain which of the three skeletons was his. Goethe confirmed the sexton's decision, from the arm-bones of that one which the sexton believed to be Schiller's, declaring, that no other man in Weimar had arms of such length. The testimony of the sexton's memory and Goethe's inference, I make bold to corroborate with the cranium, whose size and shape are in harmony with the man and poet Schiller, such as we know him from his life and writings.

——Goethe, Schiller, Wieland, Herder. They still inhabit Weimar. Once they trod its streets as flesh-and-blood men, whose daily living was a benefaction and an adornment. Now they abide in it as genii, and make the little town large by their large spiritual presence. They attend you wherever you go, sanctifying and beautifying your path by their magical potency. They beckoned me into the palace, where four rooms have been dedicated to them, one to each, whose walls are ennobled by painted scenes from their works. Walking in the park, the Grand Duke passed me with his simple equipage; but I had just come from the "Garden-House" of Goethe, and the presence of the great poet and sage was so vivid, that to me he was the living reality, and the reigning Duke went by like a phantom. I might say with the concluding lines of the beautiful, touching dedication to Faust,—

> Was ich besitze seh' ich wie im weiten,
> Und was verschwand wird mir zu wirklichkeiten.*

The great dead are the most living inhabitants of Weimar. The town was to me a cemetery, and each house in it a sepulchre, which sent forth by day instead of by night, its coated or gowned ghost. The time best to enjoy the company of Weimar's high inmates, were midnight, when the present generation being in their tombs, one would be free from their petty intrusion. But at that solemn hour the wearied traveller sleeps, and if perchance he dreams, his visions are apt to be more dyspeptic than poetic.

* What I possess I see as in the distance,
And what is gone comes back in firm consistence.

CHAPTER XI.

EISENACH—THE WARTBURG—LUTHER.

ON our way back from Weimar to Frankfort, we stopped at Eisenach, that we might go up to the Wartburg, and look out over the wooded hills and valleys of Thuringia, from the same window through which Martin Luther daily looked for ten months. In this little room, himself a prisoner, he kept on at his sublime work, the liberation of Christendom from papal imprisonment. Here, plying his sinewy pen, he wrote those words which Richter calls half battles; and taking off from the Bible the Latin cloak wherewith priestcraft had hitherto concealed it, he clothed it in warm, homely German, which the newly invented types snatched up, and poured by tens of thousands upon his awakening, spirit-hungered countrymen.

Pause we a few moments on the Wartburg, while we recall the early life of this wonderful man. The best monuments of men are their lives, and those of our benefactors we never tire of contemplating. In their self-written inscriptions there is an enduring significance. We are fortified by coming near to their greatness. It is a profitable curiosity that pries into the modest beginnings of men whose matured lives have swollen to so broad a current, that they inundate the history of their kind. Only the greatest rivers are eagerly traced to their source.

The boy out of whom grew the gigantic man, Martin Luther, once begged in the streets of the town there beneath us, singing before houses to earn bread, as was the custom then in Germany for poor school-boys. Dame Ursula, widow of John Schweichard, taking pity on the child, gave him a home in her house, and kept him at school in Eisenach for four years, after which he entered the University at Erfurth, where his father was then able to support him. "Luther," says Michelet, "writes of his benefactress with words of emotion, and on her account showed gratitude towards women all his life."

Luther's father was a worker in mines. Like other peasants of that day, some of whom, in imitation of their seignorial masters, adopted armorial bearings, John Luther took for his arms a hammer. This symbol of his humble trade was prophetic of the vocation of his son, for Martin proved to be a hammerer whose blows, struck with the boldness of a martyr and the force of a Titan, reshaped Christendom. He hammered Catholicism out of its catholicity ; he broke its universality. With the mighty sledge-hammer of reason, he knocked half the limbs off of the Pope, who since that hops on one leg.

Luther was destined for the law ; but like all men in whom are conjoined a large soul with a large intellect, the study of what has been falsely termed the "reason of humanity." had for him no attraction. Literature and music were his delight. "Music," he says, "is the art of prophets ; it is the only one which, like theology, can calm the troubles of the soul, and put the devil to flight." He seems to have had feeling for Art ; he was the friend of the famous German painter, Lucas Cranach. The early spontaneous tendencies always denote important elements in the nature of a man. The geniality which in Luther underlay the dogmatic theologian and brawny combatant, was an ingredient of his greatness.

The more powerful the nature, the less is it liable to be directed by circumstances. A warm, vigorous mind makes new circumstances as a medium for itself, and resists the old ones. This initiative potency is the source of progress in the world. But the strongest cannot wholly withdraw himself from the action of outward pressure, nor even from the controlling effect of single events. Luther had just entered manhood, when the current of his life received a new direction from a startling incident. One of his companions was struck dead at his side by a flash of lightning. In his terror he made a vow to St. Anne to become a monk if he escaped. Fourteen days later, after having spent the evening gaily with friends in making music, he entered at midnight the monastery of the Augustines in Erfurth, carrying with him nothing but Plautus and Virgil. It was two years before his father would be resigned to this his son's self-immolation. At the end of that time he consented to be present at Martin's ordination. A day was chosen when the poor miner could leave his work, and he brought with him and gave to his lost child all the money he had laid by, twenty florins.

There is beauty in this early passage in the life of Luther. That he should have kept a vow taken at such a moment, is proof of his truthfulness and his resolution. In the act there was fidelity and strength. Then, the grief of the father, ending in the bestowal on the son of all his savings. One rejoices to meet with touching facts like this in the early life of a great man. Such are always to be found where men are manly and true-hearted, and it is by the substance out of which they spring that greatness is nourished.

To turn monk is for a man to abdicate his humanity. He truncates himself of his upper endowments. He extinguishes the higher lights of life, those that are fed by the sympathies of labor and of love. He cuts the myriad threads that, binding him to his fellows, are the sole means of unfolding and fortifying his manhood. Thus isolated, the mind,—which can not be totally stifled,—preys upon itself. The monk is abandoned to a moral self-defilement. He dwindles to be the shadow of a man, or he bloats out to be a beast with feeding for his chief work. Luther could not stay monk, but his initiation into a monastery was for himself and for Christendom an immense event: it was decisive of his career. Monk-like, he preyed upon himself, but thereby a stirring was given to his deep nature. In the terrible tussles of the spirit, light went up in him that otherwise had probably smouldered forever. He stumbled upon a neglected Bible. Conceive of Luther, with a conscience as inexorable as Radamanthus, an intellect like St. Paul's, unaided by other human insight or sympathy, imprisoned with unthinking, unbelieving monks, unlocking the Book. There was food and an appetite! Job and Isaiah, and David and St. Paul first made known to Luther. We are now familiar with the Bible. On entering manhood we find ourselves possessed of its substance without knowing how we have come by it. The Bible is a universal heir-loom in protestant families. But in 1505 it was a sealed book. If a few learned recluses had read it, they had merely read it; it fructified not in them for their or others' profit. Were a cohort of Angels to come singing from the Heavens visibly and audibly celestial symphonies in our ears, we should hardly be more amazed than was Luther, as his deep eager spirit suddenly found itself in full communion with the inspired singers and sages of the Old and New Testaments, their large solemn souls receiving his as the ocean receives a turbid great river, which there finds calm and transparency.

In the monastery Luther had his first great lesson. He learnt there faith, not from his brother monks, who had none, but from his own thirsting spirit that had found its mate in the grand, fiery soul of St. Paul.

Without faith a man is not a full man. By self-reliance a strong man can do much, but to do the most, to self-reliance he must add reliance on the HIGH. "Things hoped for" must become "substance" to his eyes by the intensity of his belief in

Good. Into such strength are his powers knit up by this spiritual attraction, that he is then, and only then, ready and fit for greatest undertakings.

In the providential schooling that Luther went through to train him for his destined task, the second lesson was his journey to Italy. Had his heart not been opened in the monastery, his eyes would not have been opened to see what was to be seen in Italy. The poor Augustin Monk set out on foot, full of joy and hope and spiritual life. On the way he was harbored at the monasteries of his order. Coming down from the mountains upon Milan, he was there received into a monastery of marble and seated at a sumptuous table. He passed from monastery to monastery, that is, from palace to palace. Venturing once to tell some Italian monks that they would do better not to eat meat on Friday, this freedom nearly cost him his life. Astounded, saddened, the single-minded German pursued his foot-journey through the burning plains of Lombardy. He arrived ill at Padua; still he would not halt, but pushed on and reached Bologna almost dying. Restored to health, he hurried forward, traversed Florence without stopping, and at last entered Rome. He fell on his knees, raised his hands to Heaven, and cried out, "Hail, holy Rome, sanctified by the holy martyrs, and by their blood which has been shed in thee." In his fervor he ran from one holy spot to another, saw everything, believed everything. He soon discovered that he believed alone. He was in Rome, but Christian Rome no more.

The fallen Marius, seated on the ruins of Carthage, was a less sublime spectacle than the erect Luther in Rome, amidst the ruins of the Christian faith. One spiritually-minded priest, amid that sensual throng; one living soul, amid all those deadened souls; one believer, amid Rome's mitred scoffers; one humble, God-trusting man, amid haughty atheists. What a sublime thing is the mind of a true strong man! In that festering darkness shone,—invisible then and there,—a spark of living fire, from the which was to be kindled a light that would illuminate and re-warm Christendom.

At the end of fourteen days Luther quitted Rome. He fled as from a town smitten by the plague. He says: "I would not for a hundred thousand florins not have seen Rome. I should have been troubled for fear that I did the Pope injustice."

When Tetzel, the papal vendor of Indulgences in Germany, having to the long list of orthodox sins added crimes and infamies of his own imagining, perceived his auditory struck with horror, he declared with *sang froid*, "Well, all this is expiated the moment the sound of hard cash rings in the strong-box of the Pope." In this announcement the Dominican church-broker embodied in the most transparent formula what gets to be the aim of all Hierarchies. They traffic in souls for gold and dominion. Through hopes and fears, stimulated by their fictions, they draw from men's pockets the money wherewith to consolidate their power, and then use their power to get more money.

After the Roman the richest church in Christendom, is the Anglican; and it is so because it is, after Rome, the best organized. The recent schism sprang from an effort at a still tighter organization, and this unavoidably brought the Pusey party nearer to Rome. Organization as applied to a Church involves independence of the People. By organization the Priesthood gets a permanent existence above, aside of, more or less independent of, the masses, according to the completeness of the organization. This independence, isolation and organic self-subsistence feeds ambition and encourages the impudent blasphemous assumption of especial God-derived sanctity.

The moral duties of priests are well or ill performed, according to the moral atmosphere of each country. *But the good that priests do, they do as men not as priests.* And the richer they are as priests the less good will they do as men.

The acme of priestly greed, impudence, and imposture, is the selling of Indulgences,—a practice by no means yet disused.

At the time that Tetzel commenced the sale of indulgences in Germany Luther was Doctor in Theology, Professor in the University of Wittemberg, provincial vicar of the Augustines, and charged with the functions of the Vicar General in the pastoral visits to Misnia and Thuringia. He was high in place, of great consideration and influence. But he was one of those true men upon whom high trusts impose high duties. Indignant at this vile traffic, he applied to his Bishop, praying him to silence Tetzel. The Bishop answered him, that he had better keep silent himself. He then wrote to the Primate, the Archbishop of Mayence, but distrusting him, on the same day that he despatched his letter he affixed to the Castle-Church of Wittemberg his celebrated propositions.

A great truth or idea is something so deep and subtle, even when most simple, that the great man who announces it conceives not its full import. He is the depositary of a germ from the Universal, the which he is commissioned to plant and to till, but it is a new seed, and to what it will grow he cannot foresee. But ideas once planted by man are watered and nourished by Providence, for Providence doth ever countenance genius. A far bolder and broader act than Luther himself knew was the publication of those propositions. Striking at the most accursed of tyrannies, that over the mind, he opened a breach through which by gradual enlargements man was to come out from all prisons, civil as well as ecclesiastical, out of royal bondage into republican liberty, out of Lutheranism itself as well as out of Romanism,—such progressive life is there in truth. Not only were the immense historical after-consequences of his first act necessarily invisible to Luther, but so vigorous and rapid was its fecundation that its effects upon his contemporaries astounded him. Upon no one did it work more potently than upon himself. Of the emancipation of his own mind, not only from papal but from regal authority, brought about, unconsciously to himself, by the working of his first great anti-papal act, there is lively evidence in the new treasonable freedom wherewith he soon after wrote of Princes. He says of them ;—"You ought to know that from the beginning of the world a prudent Prince is a very rare thing, rarer still an upright Prince. They are generally great fools or great reprobates."*

It was on the 31st of October, 1517, that Luther affixed to the Castle-Church of Wittemberg his propositions.

Since the first day of the Christian era there had been in human annals no day so pregnant, so solemn as this. To Americans especially this day ought to be holy. Without it there had not been that other memorable epoch-marking day, the 4th of July, 1776. On the 31st of October, 1517, was made to the world the Declaration of Mental Independence. Upon Germany, upon Europe, it fell like a trumpet-tongued summons from a better world. Luther found himself hostilely arrayed against the Pope. That was a fearful position. Even the great Luther shrank back; and had he not had above his strong intellect a conscience that would know no compromise of principle, and behind it a courage that could brave all the Powers of Earth and Hell, he would have succumbed. In the middle of the 19th century we can scarcely conceive what strength, what moral grandeur that man must have had, who, in the beginning of the 16th defied the authority of the Pope. Luther did defy it steadfastly. He asserted the spiritual self-sufficiency, the moral dignity of man. By all freemen he should be revered as one of their mightiest deliverers. Noble, stout-hearted Brother; we thank thee for thy great courage, we thank thee for thy great intellect, and above all we thank thee for thy great conscience.

* The truthfulness of Luther's picture of Princes has lately been acknowledged in Prussia, where a volume selected from his writings, containing his opinions of them, was burnt by order of government. Luther burnt in protestant Germany! What a close hug Kingcraft and Priestcraft are giving each other to strengthen themselves against Democracy.

CHAPTER XII.

WHO FOLLOWED LUTHER—RACES—COLOR—CHRISTIANITY—PROTESTANTS AND CATHOLICS—ENGLISH AND SPANISH AMERICA—CONVERSIONS TO ROMANISM—RELIGION.

It is of deep historic interest to note, who followed Luther in this vast stride; who in that age was capable of being freed from the yoke of sacerdotal usurpation.

"O! the difference of man and man,"

cries Goneril. So different are men, that there never were two just alike; and at the same time all are so alike, that we must acknowledge the cannibal for our brother. Nations,—organic multitudes geographically defined,—like the individuals whereof they are composed, likewise differ one from the other. Races, too,—numbered by naturalists at from three to six, each embracing many nations,—differ broadly in aptitudes, habits, manners, physiognomy, color. This last quality, color, be it observed, is not a mere superficial mark, but denotes deep differences, being an index of mental capacity. At one end of the human scale is the black man, at the other the white, between them the brown and yellow. The white man never comes into contact and conflict with the others that he does not conquer them. The brown and yellow he subjugates or exterminates, the black he holds in bondage. The two extremes meet in this close union.* In color

* They who, assuming for themselves a pre-eminence in philanthropy, run into such extremes of opinion and indignation, because their white

there is great significance. Nature is never arbitrary, nor shallow, nor illogical. She would not stamp one man white, another brown, another black, and mean nothing thereby, or no more than surface-diversity as among cattle or flowers. White and black—light and darkness—these are deep words. Whence is it that the white is always at the top of the scale of humanity, the yellow in the middle, and the black at the bottom? Not of choice, not of outward influences are these pervading, enduring facts the result, but of law and inward motions.

None but nations of the white race, and only a few of these, have a civil, a political history; that is, a development and the record thereof. History implies growth, that is, childhood, youth, maturity. National growth implies depth and a fund of resources. In the current of centuries, a people of high organization unfolds itself from within, until it reaches a refined multiplex life. Slowly it traverses degrees, planting itself on its advancements still to ascend. Its annals are written in comprehensive institutions that fortify its progress, and in monuments, not merely solid and enduring, like the Pyramids of Egypt,—for that were not enough,—but deriving their durability from their instructiveness, like the statuary and architecture of Greece, and the books of the Hebrews, Greeks, and Romans,—statues and books that still live, not because they reflect the thoughts and deeds of those nations, but because in their thoughts and deeds was the vitality that springs from the beauty there is in truth, and the truth there is in beauty. These three are the only nations of Antiquity that were nervous enough to create history, and therefore the only ones from whom the moderns have learnt.

In each of them, be it noted, the democratic spirit was strong, but only partially developed; for its full unfolding, Christianity

brothers hold by inheritance their black brothers in bondage, let them look discerningly into Natural History. The search may have the effect of enlarging the range of their fraternal solicitude.

was needed,—Christianity, which is the highest moral generalization; which would substitute charity for force, broad faith for petty hopes, justice for expediency.

The other races, ancient or modern, the colored, have not in them the spring for indefinite progressiveness, for God-clasping development, no upward yearning for moral or intellectual generalization. Feeble on their path are the traces of beauty or wisdom; shrivelled or immature their intellectual fruit. They have no ripe art, no great books, no history. They are not expansive, not creative. They cannot clear the circle of animal littleness. They lie bound in the sterility of savageism, or the immobility of barbarism: their life is an intellectual and moral pauperism. They are unfinished, and according to both history and philosophy,—whose testimony when concurrent is clenching,—destined not to be finished.

When we use the phrase, "the great cause of humanity;" when we speak of man as capable of being indefinitely enlarged by thought and invention, and exalted by poetry and sentiment; when we triumph in the growth of science and culture, our words, whether or not we will it or know it, apply only to the white race. History declares that the only æsthetic, the only scientific man, is the white man.

Christianity is confined to the white race, and does not embrace all that. This is an enormous fact in the natural history of man. Christianity involves a struggle of man to put himself under the rule of his highest sentiments. Only the white race has had the inward impetus, the conscious need, the swelling vitality to make this struggle, to escape from the tyranny of sensualism into the upper region of possible liberty where predominates the spiritual.

Christianity, promising the reign of justice, leads to liberty, for men can only get to freedom through the dominion of their noblest faculties. It has been a path for going forward and upward. Upon this path mankind could only enter after it had reached a certain growth. Far ahead of all others on the earth are those nations that entered it. They and only they have gone continuously forward. Where they have not, is owing partly to this—that the spirit of Christianity—the aspiration for a higher life—has been smothered by ecclesiastical usurpation. In the 14th and 15th centuries, after ages of priestly tyranny and sophistication, it had got to be so smothered. Wickliffe, Huss, Jerome of Prague, Savonarola re-uttered this spirit to priest-ridden Christendom, and prepared its soul to hearken to Luther.

To some nations are allotted high functions in the life of Humanity. In ancient times the Hebrews, the Greeks, the Romans, predominated in turn over the race. In modern history, Italy emerged first out of the mediæval darkness. Among the Italians there was, in the 13th and three following centuries, a revival of the Greek and Roman genius. In the struggle for emancipation from ecclesiastical dominion, commenced by Wickliffe, and triumphantly conducted by Luther, the German breed led the way. The Reformation embraced northern and central Germany, Sweden, Denmark, Holland, and Great Britain, all belonging to the German family. In mixed France it took deep root, but did not gain over openly more than one eighth of the whole population. In Spain and Italy the priesthood was too strong, and manhood then too weak for it even to take root. In Poland it scarcely got a footing. In the Austrian dominions, out of a population of thirty-five millions, but three millions two hundred thousand are protestants. In Switzerland, more than half the inhabitants are protestant.

The place held among nations, at the time that Luther put forth his propositions, by Spain, who rejected them, is now held by England, who accepted them. It is no longer the petty Queen of Spain, it is the mighty Queen of England, that can say, "The sun sets not in my dominions." Like the Ariel of her Shakspeare, England has put a girdle round the globe. The influence upon the thought of Christendom exercised by Italy through her Dantes, her Machiavellis, her Galileos, in the 15th and 16th centuries, has been, in the 18th and 19th, transferred to the Goethes, the Niebuhrs, the Hegels of Germany. Protestant Holland shook off the dominion of Spain, and erected herself into an independent Republic, that for a time disputed the sovereignty of the seas with growing England, and was strong enough to resist the power of Louis XIV. Catholic Belgium remained subject to Spain. Where are the colonies founded in America by Spain and Portugal and by Englishmen? The Protestant United States, in power and influence, take rank beside the first nations of Europe. If a people, like a man, is prosperous and strong in proportion to the number, variety, elevation and vigor of its thoughts and sensations, which are the parents of deeds, the life of the United States for fifty years exhibits such an unprecedented growth and success in all departments of human activity, as to entitle them to claim a place, not beside, but in front of all the nations of the earth. To the spirit which made Protestantism, that is, the spirit of individual liberty, of manly independence, we owe this progress and unexampled welfare. What is Mexico, or Brazil, or Bolivia? What part do they play in the stirring, striving, Christian community? What conquests are they making in the domains of Nature—what fruitful secrets do they wrest from her deep heart? What discourse is heard among them of great human interests? New ideas, winged thoughts, what acceptance do they find among the nations of South America? Ask their oracles, their priests.

In France the massacre of St. Bartholomew and the revocation of the edict of Nantes tell the strength of Protestantism, and with what dread it filled tyrants. At this moment hardly the half of Frenchmen can be claimed by Rome. With the mass, Catholic observances are a habit rather than a faith. Among the educated there is an almost universal religious disbelief in the Church, coupled with a political belief in it as an engine for keeping the people ignorant and dependent; and for this end it is the most efficient apparatus that human ingenuity stimulated by human egotism could devise. The French Revolutions that have pulled down the throne and set up man, have shaken the altar and put God in the place of the Pope.

In Italy the open profession of dissent from the Romish Church is not tolerated. But those who, despising its mummeries and hating its extortionate tyranny, reject in their hearts as well its spiritual as its temporal assumptions, are to be numbered by millions. Let Italy become independent, and there will be revealed a sum of Protestantism, of protesters against Priestcraft, a tithe of which will counterbalance the trumpeted conversions to Romanism from among the idle, ennuied "Nobility and Gentry" of England.

Conversions* to Catholicism in Protestant countries should in most cases be looked upon as a throwing out of morbid particles, a salutary moral crisis. People who, brought up in the light of Protestantism, feel too weak to bear that light, why let them in God's name retreat and shield themselves in darkness. Liberally speaking, these losses are a gain. We want to go forward, and these good souls have not even the self-supporting life to stand upright; they must go back for support out of themselves. Peace go with them.

In this survey of Protestant and Catholic nations, what presents itself as the most striking contrast between them? It is this, that not one of the purely Catholic is independent. Popery, which, as an Italian writer says, "is a Theocracy founded on the absolutely moral slavery of man," destroying individual independence, undermines national. Italy, the fountain-head of

* These conversions, be it noted, are chiefly from the Church of England, which has features of likeness to that of Rome. To weak minds, or to those that to a sensuous quality of intellect unite a peculiar sentimental organization, the transition from Anglicanism to Romanism is logical.

Catholicism, where Protestantism is proscribed under penalty of imprisonment or death, has been for centuries a prey to the foreigner. Portugal, as Catholic as Italy, the favorite torture-house of the Inquisition, is a dependence of Protestant England. Spain, where by a late concordat the ban against Protestantism has been renewed, is so helpless, that she had within thirty years to call in a French army under the Duc d'Angoulême to uphold the tottering Bourbon throne, and having lost nearly all her immense colonies, is now obliged to appeal to England and France to prevent the last remaining one from falling into our hands. Poland,—blotted from the list of nations. Austria,—saved lately from destruction by the sword of Russia. Ireland,—compare Ireland with Scotland. France, vigorous, independent France, has not only four or five millions of Protestants, but how many millions besides of Voltairiens, until lately, when Skepticism, which is by the nature of man short-lived, having passed away, Socialism, or a belief in man involving a deeper belief in God, is begetting a higher Christianity than has yet animated Christendom, —a Christianity destined to be far more fruitful than ever was the theological, the which however is now everywhere almost as good as dead.

But deeper and stronger than either, than Catholicism, than Protestantism, both perishable, is the imperishable Christian principle of liberty, the quenchless longing for absolute mental freedom. Protestantism was the assertion of this principle against the usurpation of Rome. It was a conflict for truth, but not itself the broadest truth, that it could not be; a struggle for emancipation, but not itself the largest liberty, that it could not be. It quickly put bounds to its own essence, the right of private judgment, of free inquiry; it narrowed itself to *isms*. It is not universal in its embrace; it is partial, and thus runs into Sectarianism. It has no Pope, but it has creeds; it has no monasteries, but it has theological seminaries; it has no independent hierarchy (except in England), but it has dogmatic priesthoods. In its churches ecclesiastical abuses are vastly mitigated, by no means fully abated. Protestantism has its army of priests, who are, too many of them, Jewish in their narrowness and their hates, and in their assumptions papal; and who, if they could, would, like their Romish colleagues, persuade us that priests are essential to salvation, the very depositaries and dispensers of spiritual life, the indispensable bond to unite men to God. In this they serve themselves more than God and men. When a man places himself between God and another man, he intercepts the light and casts a shadow upon his brother. He is a false priest who would make himself indispensable to men as a medium of union with God. The true priest aims to unfold the soul, and thus disclose to it its own innate powers and grandeur.

A primary and pre-eminent element of our mental being is religion. To say of a man, he is without religion, is as much nonsense as to say he is without lungs. Breathing is not more essential to the physical life than is to the moral a recognition of the Infinite, a reverential consciousness of the Absolute and Unspeakable. So sophisticated are men's minds by one-sided teachings, that they come to regard religion as a something they get from the priest, a spiritual treasure guarded and dispensed by the priesthood. At stated periods they go to Church to receive their share of it, like stockholders to the Bank to draw their dividends. They have made an investment in the Church and leave the management thereof to the priests, who pay them in prayers, sermons and liturgies. In this way forms usurp the place of substance, dead material husk of spiritual kernel.

As are the temperament and the moral and intellectual wants of a people so are its divinities, who are modified, aye moulded, by the mental characteristics of each. Hence the difference between the Gods of the Greeks and the God of the Hebrews, between the worship of the Hindoo and that of the African. Men can only conceive God according to their own capacities. To the low man ever a low God. As individual men in their narrowness would have other men like themselves, so aggregate men, men in tribes and nations make God like man. Anthropomorphism is the egotism of unemancipated humanity. Through culture and moral enlargement we attain to the conception of he vitalizing omnipresent Deity as incorporeal essence. As man rises, the Deity shines the more purely upon his heart, God and man exalting one another. To the upstriving man the Deity holds out a helping hand, ascending ever higher and higher, the more and more effulgent with intellect and love as man mounts after him towards the centre of Liberty and Truth, the eternal home of the infinite Good.

Jesus, an inmate of this heavenly home, from the depths of his large soul proclaimed the law of love, justice, unity. This solemn, momentous proclamation has remained a prolific abstraction, kept present to the human soul by the inborn need of its fulfilment. Only in Jesus himself burnt purely the light of his revelation. The Apostles his agents were tainted with Judaism. And soon the spirit of priestcraft, which had crucified Jesus, took possession of his doctrine and soiled it. It is not yet purged of the soiling. The God of priestcraft is a God of wrath, inspiring fear more than love, a priest-made God to serve priestly ends of dominion; gloomy, revengeful, the oppressor not the liberator of humanity, whose messengers are oftener devils than angels. Do you purify man by defiling God with cruelty? By abasing man do you exalt God? Do you strengthen the heart by compressing it into intolerant creeds, do you shelter it under mystic imaginations? Out of trite fancies and sour sensibilities you would build up Deity, and present as the Infinite the image they make on your finite brains. In flimsy phrases you would word the Unspeakable, in fleeting vesture clothe the Eternal, and then you solemnly declare the outcome of these your theological inventions to be God, and summon us to worship as the Creator this your dwarfish misshapen creature.

What profit hath the soul from these degradations of Deity? Is it not akin to image-worship, this petrifaction of fallible interpretations into staunch creeds? Beams from the central Light deflected through Judaic imaginations, can they retain any warmth for the 19th century? What knowledge or nourishment is there now in these ancient aspirations? Is spiritual life replenished by feeding more on the man-made than the God-made? This temple built with hands, what is it to the sanctuary within the heart? This formal conned ritual, what is it to the spontaneous aspiration of the soul? What are your loud prayers and hymns to the voiceless communion with the Infinite? The silence of a Church is voiceful to the solemnity of a man's conscience! Your altars, your surplices, your mitres, your cathedrals, your consecrations, all are but verbiage and stitchwork and brickwork, ostentatious, transitory, in face of the eternal self-renewing life, the deep sacredness of the soul of man. Protestantism, one-sided and short-coming as it is, was the rehallowing of this desecrated sanctuary, the reassertion of this unacknowledged sacredness. The Reformation of the 16th century rescued men from much of their captivity to priesthood. It shattered many of the bars that made churches prisons. It is an illuminated phasis in the history of liberty, of Christian deliverance.

* The light then kindled in a few souls now shines over Christendom. From the door of the humble church in Wittemberg, where it was first set up, that light spread from land to land, from generation to generation, vivifying and fortifying wherever it fell, so that at the present day those nations that opened their hearts the widest to its rays are the foremost on the earth. But from it,

* Chapters xi. and xii. were delivered as a "Lecture on Protestantism" in Newport, R. I., in January last. On that occasion this concluding paragraphs was added.

all the peoples of Christendom, those who are struggling to achieve, as well as those who possess liberty, be they Catholic or Protestant, chiefly draw their animation. Whether in America, where to the disenthralling, life-cherishing principles of the Reformation* we owe the best of what we have done, of what we are, of what we have, including the privilege so happily habitual among us that we forget its value, the privilege I at this moment use of publicly speaking on things of universal interest my honest thought, without fear of gaol or gibbet;—whether in steadfast England, the mighty mother of nations, who owes so much of her might to her protestantism, and to her truth-loving heart that made her accept it, where together with an obsolete aristocracy and an unspiritualized church, a load of dull Dukes and carnal Bishops, there is a fund of large manhood and freedom;—whether in France, where by means of tyrannical centralization and military organization, both inherited from monarchy, a pigmy miscreant has just been enabled to enact a gigantic crime against a long-suffering but never disheartened nation;—whether in Germany, where protestant princes, faithless alike to God and man, are foully leagued with Jesuits and Cossacks to cheat and berob an enlightened, temperate, and too trustful people of what is dearest in life, a patient people, too, but who now knowing and valuing their rights, give their robbers their hate, biding the time, which must soon come, when they can give them their vengeance;—whether in Italy, bleeding, beautiful Italy, where in the north the brutal Austrian vainly strives to trample out manhood with the soldier's heel, where in the south the Bourbon, fanatic in ferocity, slaughters men like cattle, where in the centre, in majestic Rome, the Arch-despot of the world blasphemously calls himself the vicar of Christ, while, seated on a throne built of foreign bayonets fleshed in the breasts of his subjects, he gives one hand of fellowship to the man-shaped tiger of Naples, and the

* See note at the end of the Chapter.

other to the perjured traitor of France, and, encircled by greedy, lowering Cardinals, whose red robes are dyed redder in their brothers' blood, he hearkens for the secret curses of his awakened people, who ceaselessly lust for the blood of their oppressors, and ceaselessly sigh for freedom, having learnt their cruelty from their priests, and their aspirations from their own hearts.—Wherever the breath of freedom swells healthfully in man's breast, or gasps painfully in sobs and sighs; wherever men possess, or are striving for the blessings of freedom, not one in any land of Christendom, whether Catholic or Protestant, not one of these many, many millions but owes much of what he has, or of the will and courage to desire and to dare, much of his richest inheritance or his noblest resolution, to the poor German miner's son, to the moral boldness, the intellectual might of Martin Luther.

NOTE.

In a Lecture entitled "The Catholic Chapter in the History of the United States," delivered in New York in March 1852, Archbishop Hughes says,—"It is altogether untrue to assert that this is a Catholic country, or a Protestant country. It is neither. It is a land of religious freedom and equality." General usage justifies the calling of a people Catholic or Protestant, according as a large majority of its inhabitants belong to the one or the other of these religious divisions. Thus, southern Germany is called Catholic, northern Germany Protestant; Ireland Catholic, England Protestant. The United States, where only a fraction, about one tenth, of the population, is Catholic, are called, therefore, Protestant. But, apart from common parlance, what strictly authorizes a designation is, the principle which rules a country in religious matters. By this logical test, the United States are thoroughly Protestant, and the Pope's dominions in Italy thoroughly Catholic. In the United States, there are absolute religious tolerance and liberty; in papal Italy, constraint and absolute religious intolerance. Absolute intolerance is a fundamental Catholic doctrine, which is not merely preached but severely practised, as the world knows; and practised not only against Italians, but also against strangers, so that American Protestants, while in Rome, are not permitted to meet together for public worship; such outlaws and damnable heretics are they regarded by Pope and Cardinals. In this country, on the contrary, not only is there absolute religious tolerance, but so productive is this high Christian principle, that even Romish prelates here are obliged to avow it, in the teeth of the theory and practice at headquarters. Thus Archbishop Hughes, in this Lecture, "hopes that it will remain a land of religious freedom and equality to the latest posterity." On other occasions he has made like declarations. These avowals have no significance as signs of the wishes and purposes of an Archbishop; for Catholic prelates exercise—especially, we presume, when dealing with heretics—a right of mental reservation, which paralyzes any positive interpretation that the ingenuous might put on their words, and is probably large in proportion to the hierarchical elevation of the dignitary. But they have significance, as showing what is the power of Protestantism here, and what a very Protestant country Archbishop Hughes thinks it, that he, a nominee of the Pope, drawing from Rome his archiepiscopal breath, should feel obliged to reiterate so unpapal, so uncatholic a sentiment, the which he would no more utter in Rome than he would there laud Luther or deny purgatory.

"If," says the lecturer, "there had been only one form of Protestantism professed in all the colonies, I fear mucn that even with Washington at their head, the Constitution would not have been what it is in regard to religious liberty." But it is the very nature of Protestantism, when it has free play, to break a people up into many sects. The essence of Protestantism is the right of private judgment in religious belief, which right leads unavoidably and healthfully to multiplication of creeds. Protestantism is a protest against sacerdotal dominion, and the assertion of individual religious independence. It frees men from the yoke of priesthood; it empowers every man to define his own creed, to choose, or to be, his own priest. This, the fundamental principle of Protestantism, involves absolute religious liberty. That Protestant sects and men have violated this principle, proves only the fallibility of men, but shakes not the foundations of the principle itself. However uncharitable some sects in this country may have been, or may be, in their feelings towards each other, a higher law controls them—the law of Protestant freedom, which, if not complete, goes yet to the extent of guaranteeing to each man immunity from interference of State or Church, against his will, in his religious profession. Granting that the multiplicity of sects led to this general tolerance; the multiplicity of sects is the robust offspring of Protestantism, and by its excess here proves, that this country is ultra-protestant.

In a "Catholic Chapter in the History of the United States," Maryland would of course not be omitted. What right has Archbishop Hughes to say "Catholic Maryland," he who a few pages before asserts that this country is neither Protestant nor Catholic? If this country was not at first and is not now Protestant, how can Maryland be called Catholic? Among the first colonists of Maryland there were Protestants, as there were Catholics among the first colonists of the other provinces. The proportion of Protestants in the Maryland colony was at any time as large as that of Catholics in all the other colonies, or in the United States, after their independence. With his own words we contradict Archbishop Hughes' designation, and say, that Maryland "was neither Catholic nor Protestant. It was a land of religious freedom and equality."—And as such it was in its birth eminently uncatholic.

To learn what the Catholic view of a subject is, we must go to Rome, to the Pope who appoints the Archbishops Hughes, to the Cardinals who appoint the Pope. Rome is the fountain of all Catholic doctrine. Now we find that in Rome, at present, and at the time that Maryland was founded, and at all times, nothing is more abominated than this very religious liberty. "I will not, by myself or any other, directly or indirectly, molest any person professing to believe in Jesus Christ, for or in respect of religion." Such was the oath prescribed by Lord Baltimore for the Governor of his Maryland. Did he get that from Rome? Does the Pope prescribe such an oath for the Governor of his Rome? Papist or the dungeon of the Inquisition, that is the alternative of the native Roman. Torture or death awaits him who there presumes to exercise what Lord Baltimore fully and formally granted,—freedom of conscience. Not even can strangers there worship after their choice. Let a score of Maryland Protestants try it within the walls of Rome; they will find that they dare not even meet together to say their prayers. They will not be indirectly, but most "directly molested," lest by their Protestant communion the capital of Catholicism be desecrated, and Pope and Cardinals insulted and scandalized. And yet Rome's bemitred minions here, claim the founding of Maryland as Roman Catholic work!—If a Quaker were to forget the precepts of his religion, and take to swearing and fisticuffs, would the odium of his aberration fall on the whole "Society of Friends," or only on the exceptional member? If a lawgiver inserts in his code a clause in flat conflict with a fundamental dogma, an inflexible maxim, of the church to which he belongs, a clause the directly opposite of which finds place in the code of that church itself; in after-years, when this clause turns out to have been wise and creditable, is the church to claim the merit thereof, and that too when her own practice is still as hostile as ever to the very principle embodied in that clause? As the Quaker, for his unquakerly conduct is read out of meeting, so Lord Baltimore, for his official unpapal religious tolerance, would doubtless,—but for worldly considerations,—have been sentenced to do penance or to pay a round sum for absolution, if even he had not been excommunicated. For the sin of liberality (although only verbal and calculated) in this lecture and other similar occasions, Archbishop Hughes has, I dare say, penitently to mortify the flesh, or else be absolved (beforehand probably) by the Italian Prince, his master.

The original Constitution of Maryland, drafted by the Proprietor, was the work of a clear-headed, large-hearted man,—a man so strong, that, in founding a state so early as the beginning of the seventeenth century, he put at its basis the broad human rights of civil and religious liberty,—a man so Christian, that the unchristian intolerance of even the Church he had chosen, did not taint his heart. If the King who endowed him with this domain on the Chesapeake did, as has been surmised, as a Protestant, exact religious tolerance in the organization of the new government, Lord Baltimore, if this tolerance had been unpalatable to him, would have applied for lands to the King of Spain or of Portugal; and these "most Catholic" sovereigns would eagerly have granted to one so honored in England as he was, a choice tract in their rich American possessions; and there he could have established himself, like his neighbors, to his Catholic heart's content, in severest Catholic exclusiveness. But the papist was not uppermost in Lord Baltimore's nature, and therefore he had not recourse to Spain or to Portugal, and he sought not help of the Pope. The liberal clauses of his charter, so hostile to the spirit of Romanism, and so deservedly celebrated in history, were dictated by his own high human feelings; and no heretic-cursing Pope, no ambitious sophistical Archbishop, has claim to a tittle of his noble deed. The illustrious founder of Maryland belongs not to their side, but to the opposite one of humanity and freedom; and to him their eulogy is no honor.

CHAPTER XIII.

SUPPER-TABLE AT THE "HALF-MOON" IN EISENACH—ANNADALE—GRIMM'S TALES —MIGRATION WESTWARD.

In the evening the company at the supper-table of the "Half-Moon," in Eisenach, was enlivened by the news, just arrived from Cassel, of the flight of the Duke. It was the opening act of the Hesse-Cassel political melodrama, which afterwards ended unmelodramatically with the triumph of the guilty and the fall of the innocent. Except that the end is not yet, and will only be after that the whirlwind,—which ere long will envelop all Germany in gloom and terror,—shall have passed over, and from the bosom of the enfranchised people shall have arisen a higher justice than has ever yet presided over German affairs.

As I have generally found this summer at German Inns,—except those of fashionable watering-places,—the majority of the little circle at the "Half-Moon" was democratic. The discussion of the doings in Cassel was conducted with vivacity, but with good temper. One of the speakers was the head-waiter, who, without either forwardness or timidity, took part in the conversation, and expressed moderate opinions in good language, performing at the same time his duties round the table with watchfulness and alacrity. The spirit of the great Wartburg prisoner, that animates so many millions all over the globe, had made a man of this humble servant.

The traveller through Eisenach should take two or three hours,

—whether he has them to spare or not,—to visit Annadale. After a drive of two miles through a beautiful valley, you enter on foot a narrow winding gorge, whose rocky sides are embowered by overhanging trees, under which you walk on a gravel path not wide enough for two abreast. But what constitutes the peculiar beauty of the place, and marks it as a unique natural curiosity, is the fine moss on the rocks, covering them as completely and as smoothly as if silk velvet had been carefully fitted on them by feminine fingers, and kept of the most vivid green by the shade of the forest and the moisture from springs.

It is a place to tell fairy tales in. With such poetry before the senses, the mind grows fantastic. So much beauty should not be wasted on solitude; it solicits you to people it. One can readily conceive how an imaginative race like the Germans should, in their robust youth, have populated the dells of their virgin forests with fays and fairies. These attended the Saxons to England, where Shakspeare by adopting, after educating them, has given them an everlasting home.

Of the safety wherewith traditions travel down through many generations, with no other vehicle than the tongues of nurses and grandmothers, I had, while a student at Göttingen, a remarkable exemplification. One of the Grimms had just published a collection of children's stories all gathered by himself from the mouths of aged women,—chiefly in the Hartz Mountains. In looking through them I came upon one that was in its minute and absurd particulars precisely the same tale that I had heard as a child in America. A thousand years ago it had gone over to England, had there lived from mouth to mouth through thirty generations, had then traversed the Atlantic and dwelt for two hundred years near the shores of the Chesapeake, and now, brought thence packed away in the memory of an American, back to its starting-place, was found, after having changed its vesture from Gothic to Anglo-Saxon, and from Anglo-Saxon to English, to match as accurately a tale now for the first time printed, as one proof-sheet does another taken from the same form of types. In rude Gothic the two had parted more than ten centuries ago, and now met, the one in German, the other in English, and in the many vicissitudes of that long separation, neither had changed a feature.

It were curious to seek the origin of these tales in the East. The affinities of language and similarities in many words point to the neighborhood of the Caspian Sea as the cradle of the German tribes. To some of the many inquisitive travellers, who are eager for new fields of exploration, here is a captivating enterprise, to penetrate to that region and bring away the popular and nursery tales as philological and ethnographical treasures.

Tradition and researches do not entirely concur with the Mosaic record in placing the origin of man in the East. Yet it were not unreasonable to suppose that man first appeared in the highlands of Asia because there the Earth was first humanly habitable. From what is now observed and known, we are authorized to infer, that the whole surface of the Earth was not at once put in condition to be the abode of man. Asia may have been first ready, and America or Australia last, perhaps thousands of years later.

Facts justify the line of Bishop Berkeley that

Westward the march of Empire takes its course,

shifting its seat as the streams of population,—of white population,—pouring down from the centre of Asia towards its western confines and Europe, grew stronger and clearer the further they advanced. From Asia the march of Empire was to Greece, and thence to Italy, and from Italy still further westward to Spain, France, England. Driving ever westward, population followed Columbus across the stormy Atlantic, and founded on its American shore an Empire that will as much exceed England in power as England does Rome in Rome's proudest day, and as Rome herself did the Assyrian monarchy in its broadest magnificence. But America had already been peopled. This population, coming out of Asia eastward, was met and driven back again towards Asia by that which came out of Asia through Europe westward, and is destined to be extinguished by the latter.

That it is a law of Nature that migration should "go with the sun," we have startling proof in this fact, that the aboriginal inhabitants of America, who in peopling that Continent had violated this law, are thus thrust back by those who obeyed it. This, it may be said, is only the superior white subjecting the inferior brown race. In India too the white man has subjected the brown, but he has not overflowed his territory and displaced him. The British and Dutch Indies are held by a handful of whites through military possession. So the English, who have set an armed foot in China, may subdue it as they have subdued Hindostan. But the peopling of the eastern shore of Asia with swarms from the great white hive, is to take place by migration westward, that is, from Oregon and California.

The strong, the white race, streamed westward; the western Asiatics are to this day white. Those who from the region which according to Oriental tradition is given as the starting-place of mankind went eastward, the Chinese, the Siamese, the Japanese, belong to the inferior brown and yellow races. It may be objected that all having originated from one stock, the difference of color was caused by climate, food, water and other external influences. The force of these influences is undeniable; but admitting, what is by no means demonstrated, that the parents of the whole human family were a single couple, their color must remain a mystery; and therefore we cannot know whether climate re-changed brown to white in Western Asia and Europe, or white to brown and black in Eastern Asia and Africa.*

* A recent French writer, M. Henri Lecouturier, in a remarkable work,

Color, in races, is not a mere outward cutaneous painting by the sun, but comes from within, from the blood. That long action of the sun with other outward agencies will change the quality of the blood, may be believed. But a strong race may carry within itself the vigor to resist and even to reverse the effect of these agencies. In figure the Anglo-Saxons in America have as-

entitled *Cosmosophie ou le Socialism Universel*, endeavors by an ingenious exposition to prove, that the birth-place of man was in the Polar region. According to his deduction the first man was black and covered with hair, and like certain tribes still found in Africa, was nearer to the Ourang Outang than to the white man. Towards the Poles, it was that the Earth first became cool enough to be habitable; and when man first appeared, the climate there was as warm as it now is under the Equator, while that of the temperate and torrid zones was so hot as to be uninhabitable. With the receding of the Ecliptic,—which at first extended over the whole ninety degrees,—and the corresponding receding of the focal fires within the Earth, the cooling of the surface, which began at the Poles, extended gradually to the temperate zone. At the same time the polar region grew cooler and cooler, and the first men, adapted to the greater warmth, followed it and gradually approached the equator, in the heats of which their descendants are now found in Africa.

His hypothesis is, that the first man was preceded by the monkey, who went before him also in migrating towards the equatorial region, where he is still found. As the monkey left man behind him, so the first race of black hairy men left superior men their descendants behind themselves, the race improving in color and quality with the cooling of the Earth and the purification of its zones, until, after many ages of successive migrations, the inferior breeds following the heat and the superior taking their place, the whole Earth was peopled, and the highest types were found in the temperate zone and the lowest in the torrid.

The genealogy of man, says M. Lecouturier, may be learnt by beginning with the present occupants at the tropical regions and going northward. The most advanced will be found in the temperate zone, and the most backward, that is, the primitive and oldest races, in the torrid. For a general classification he divides the human family into three races, the lowest, the middle, and the highest; the Ethiopian, the Mongolian and the Caucasian; each embracing several varieties.

The Finns, Laplanders and Esquimaux, a stunted and misshapen race living on the borders of the Arctic circle, are remains of the primitive races, who refused to follow the current that drew them towards the warm latitudes. Philological researches have shown such an affinity between the Finns and the Hungarians, that Berghaus puts them down on his Ethno-

similated somewhat to the North American Indians; but who would thence conclude, that they are to grow downward to them? On two races so wide apart as these, the one having an organization so superior to that of the other, is it not reasonable to presume, that external influences, telluric and solar, magnetic and material, might act with opposite effects, weakening the weaker race and strengthening the stronger; and that thus, while the Europeans in North America, under the above influences, should come to resemble in some minor characteristics the natives, the gulf between them would in the main be widened, and the original organic superiority of the white race be not only maintained but augmented?

This proclivity of man, or rather of the white race, westward,—exhibited in subordinate movements as well as in the great cardinal migrations,—would seem to proceed from an instinct that harmonizes men unconsciously with the order of Nature. Westward is the path forward, the path of progress. Conservatism looks backward, that is, eastward. Thus at this moment, princes in Germany look with hope to Russia, in Spain to Rome; the People, with a deeper intuition, to America, and themselves. On the other hand, Russia dreams of another Scythian invasion, and Rome is straining to get command of the advanced guard of humanity in America,—which she will do when printing shall be there prohibited as the abettor of crime, and steam suppressed as a disturber of the public peace, and the reasoning faculty proscribed as an obstacle to virtue,—a prohibition, suppression, and proscription practised in the papal dominions, and which the paternal chiefs of the Roman Church are making a last agonizing

graphical maps as belonging to the same tribe, thus confirming the opinion of M. Lecouturier, who says, the handsome valorous Maygars are directly descended from the poor emaciated dwarfs of the polar regions.

This curious theory of the peopling of the Earth is not in contradiction with the westward migrations, which only commenced with the white race, that is, after that all the zones of the earth were peopled.

effort to perpetuate by means of the dungeon, the hangman, and Louis Bonaparte. In the great capitals, London, Paris, Berlin, New York, the west is the chosen quarter. Is this accidental, or is it not an undesigned, instinctive conformity to the saying, "The devil take the hindmost?" a saying, the significance and sad truth of which, few people suspect.

But it is time for us to obey the westward law, and move towards the Rhine.

CHAPTER XIV.

GIESSEN—LIEBIG—MARIENBERG—PRIESNITZ—THE RHINE.

On the way back to Frankfort, we stopped for the night at Giessen. It would have been a satisfaction to have availed myself of the genial accessibility of German professors, to visit Liebig, one of the stoutest living scientific pioneers,—one of the precocious band that with the sharp edge of thought are hewing for their fellow-men paths into untrodden domains,—one of that bold brotherhood of discoverers who, in the holy privacy of the laboratory and the closet, reveal new truths by light struck from the contact of genius with Nature. But we arrived late and tired. I did not see a famous captain in the great army of progress, but at the public table of the inn I saw a private working in the cause of conservatism, with a zeal and capacity that made me wonder. This was a supper-eater, who in order to conserve his body and soul tightly together during the night, transmitted through the portal of the human temple, his mouth, into the mysterious laboratory of life, the following articles of food, each in unstinted portions, and in the order here named:—1st course—fried potatoes, sausages, sourcrout, cold tongue; 2d course—stewed pigeon, pudding, roast pig, cheese with bread and butter. For a man with a weak digestion, it was dangerous, just before bed-time, to "assist," as the French say, at the piling up into one stomach of this huge heterogeneous bulk; for the bare image of it on his sleeping brain might be enough to cause nightmare.

—— No matter how often you may have seen the Rhine, to come upon it is always an event. The renowned river is a line of beauty traced on the globe by Nature, and embellished by man. On its shores I have dwelt so much, so pleasantly, and so profitably, that whenever I return to them they give me the glad greeting of a home.

To go back to old haunts is a reduplication of life. With the skipping actualities of the fretful present mingle the silent memories of the past, like marble statues looking upon a market-place. As we came down the Rhine, we bade the docile boat turn in again to the pier of venerable Boppart, that during the latter days of September we might tarry within the walls of the solid, familiar, roomy, old convent of Marienberg. A return to its gardens, its corridors, its terraces, we enjoyed the more, because we were not now, as in years past, to work hard for bodily salvation with aid of its healing waters.

What perverse children of Nature we are. She gives us health, we quickly set about to turn her gift into disease; she promises abundance, we choose to stay poor; she offers us palaces, we burrow in hovels. In all things we are unnatural; in eating, in drinking, in our outgoings and incomings, in our labors and our pleasures, in politics, in religion, in medicine. Under the spell of a cajoling conceit, we build up codes that are false, and then maintain them by sophistry and force. Most of our life is a kicking against the pricks. For our weal we should be always naturalists. Nature contains, is the law. Whether his work be rare or daily, high or low, Nature is every man's mistress, and teacher, and helper. From the ploughman to the poet, the task is well done in proportion as she mixes in the doing. Wherein lies the excellence of Shakspeare, of Goethe, of Burns, of Wordsworth, of Molière, as well as of Galileo and Newton, as well as of Fulton and Priesnitz? In their greater fidelity to Nature. They are deeper and broader naturalists.

The discovery of the power there is in water as a curative agent, was made by Priesnitz twenty-five years ago. Since that, the methods of its application have been scientifically improved and multiplied. Trials in acute diseases, and in all curable chronic ones, a thousand times repeated, have proved its efficacy. And yet this truth, so large and simple and fruitful, this balm-laden truth, is accepted by but a fraction of reading, reasoning white men. Custom, prejudice, interest, routine, timidity, conspire to retard its acknowledgment. The poisoning pill-box and life-draining lancet, keep on decimating and maiming the race. "Business before truth," is one of the mottoes of civilization, and so the blood-and-drug doctors continue in trade, and out of nature.

But let us seek comfort in retrospection. A hundred years ago the discovery of Priesnitz, like other discoveries that too far outrun their age, had probably died in its cradle. Men do reason more than they used to; knowledge does circulate more briskly and widely; truth has some service of the electric telegraph.

—— The choice spots of the globe for lounging, the one in winter and spring, the other in summer and early autumn, are the Boulevards of Paris and the Rhine; the one the work of man assisted by nature, the other the work of nature enriched by man; for a fog or a rain disenchants the Boulevards, and without its towns and villages and castles and man-movement on flood and shore, the Rhine were not the Rhine. In midsummer the valleys that run back draw you into their shades; later, you quit the stream for the heights; but always the zest of the walk is when you issue out again upon the river, and to saunter along its margin is what one does oftenest. If you are alone, you have company in the peasantry tilling or gathering in the precious narrow slopes between the water and the precipice, in the wayfarers on the smooth road, in the white-shining villages on either shore, in the old castles that solemnly address you from rock-founded eminences like spectres half-protruded from their tombs, in the freight-craft and the persevering horses that drag them against the swift current, in the steam-driven boats that queen it over the river they have conquered, and in the old river himself, a companion of infinite resources, of unfading freshness. Should you wish to rest, and from prudence prefer an indoor seat to one on a pile of macadamized stones, you enter the quiet inn of a village and call, not for a half-bottle of wine, but for a "spezialen." A "spezialen" is a small tumbler-full, and costs a groschen, about two and a half cents. This, for the privilege of resting, an hour if you choose, even should the chair-bottom be of walnut, is cheap,—provided you don't drink the wine. If you are thirsty, drink grapes, and I know not a more epicurean contrivance than to walk yourself into a summer thirst of a September afternoon on the Rhine, and then at sunset to be turned into a vineyard to slake it with purple bunches fast plucked with your own hand from the stalk.

The Rhine! The Rhine! so sweet he smells
  When buds the perfumed grape in June.
Still dearer is his shade when swells
  The rippling breeze at summer's noon.
But dearest when young Autumn's Sun
  Wipes the late dew from purpled vine,
And pours his ripening heats upon
  The spicy juice of pendant wine.

CHAPTER XV.

COLOGNE—DUSSELDORF—ARTISTS—LEUTZE'S WASHINGTON—FREILIGRATH.

Railroads and Commerce have put new life under the dying ribs of Cologne. The lazy, dirty old town, that fifty years ago offended the nostrils of Coleridge to the point of versification, has grown busy, and thence more cleanly. Whoever has the æsthetic sense would be robbed of a rightful enjoyment, if in passing through Cologne even for the twentieth time he were not allowed to stop, just to breathe for a few moments under the shadow of the Cathedral, the atmosphere of sublimity wherein that mighty torso of architectural art isolates itself. This is one of those great objects that so swell the mind with high emotion that possession eclipses hope. In this presence we are satisfied; our contentment with the hour is brimming; we are not driven forward or backward into time to fill the void we carry about in us. For mostly, the now is so flat and sour, that, horsed on the winged steeds of memory or of imagination, we fly to the far past or further future, to seek the pleasure we find not in the dull world we have built, and built with splendid materials, like senseless architects, who erecting a Palace should hide their marble and Mosaics in the foundation, and show above-ground only burnt clay and painted pine.

The pleasures of memory and imagination are satires on present life, which is so poor, that we are forever running away from it, and betaking ourselves to the deceased past and the unborn future. In childhood we sigh for the stature and exemptions of youth ; in youth we count the years and months that bar us from the liberties of manhood ; in manhood we strain forward towards age on the untiring hack, Ambition ; in maturity we strive to comfort ourselves with reminiscences of youth and childhood, that come back upon us like chiding cherubs. We are always hurrying out of to-day to get into to-morrow. We would subordinate this world to the next, and we employ at great cost a numerous class to teach us to give precedence to the world to come. We drink, and smoke, and read novels, to stave off the pressing hour. We thus make time our enemy instead of our ally—time, the flapping of whose wings are the pulses of universal life, whose hours are the foot-prints of forward-marching Eternity, and mark the unresting labors of the all-sustaining God ; labors, which it is our transcendent privilege to share, so prodigally, so divinely are we endowed.

—— Düsseldorf is an hour by railroad below Cologne, a neat, shady town, noted for its school of Art. A small city such as Düsseldorf, which becomes the seat of artists, pictures itself to you like one of those fine engraved heads of Poets encircled with a laurel garland. It stands in your mind crowned with the symbol of poetic triumph. The art-element, is not here, as in large capitals, an ingredient commingled and diluted with other superiorities ; it reigns in sole sovereignty, a sovereignty as benignant as that of light over darkness. Here are assembled a hundred men who have dedicated themselves to Beauty. To incarnate the spirit that pervades the two worlds, the world opened to ocular sense and that revealed to the eye of the mind, this is their life's thought, aim, desire, act. Through Nature and History, through all lands and activities, through the densities of the real, and the sunny pomps of the ideal, wherever thought or sense can stretch, they range in chase of Beauty, who flies from them as the maiden from the wooer whose love she would quicken by her coyness. Wherever a high deed has been done, wherever men have sacrificed themselves for mankind, wherever the higher law has gained a victory, wherever through the impulses of generous natures poetry has become act, wherever the countenance of History is agitated by great changes, there the artists gather. From the flowers of being they suck food for the nurture of their souls, that they may fulfil their high function, which is, to second God in keeping the world replenished with beauty.

The work-rooms of artists are among the pleasant places of the earth; they are green spots in our desert of prosaic life. In them you get the repose of disinterested sensations. You are drawn out of your little self into your large self. You are, moreover, as guest, in the happiest position towards the host; you partake of a double, nay, a threefold hospitality; for the man welcomes you, and the artist entertains you, and the picture greets you, it may be with a peal of celestial clarions. Between the artist and his creation is a privileged standpoint; through you he sends his thought to his work, which on its part beams with its fullest light in its master's presence. You stand as when gazing at a dewy landscape, and behind you the rising sun that has just brought it out of darkness.

After the day's work, the painters at Düsseldorf assemble towards evening in a garden on the edge of the town. The relaxation of fencing, and archery, and tenpins, in the open air, is something; but that each one will meet a score or two of his fellows, this is the spur that, pricking each one, drives scores to the daily gathering. Men are so sociable, so human; without the rays from one another's faces they could not keep warm. Here in their club the artists chat, and drink the drink made of hops, which even on the Rhine is more relished than that from the grape, and smoke, and play at games.

"Manly games," is a phrase of universal acceptation. I deny its fitness, and affirm, that when men shall be more manly they will have no games. They will then have put away childish things. Montaigne says that "sport is the work of children." Fourier says, that for young and old, work may become sport. One of the easy miracles of scientific socialism will be to make men rejoice in labor, and drawing even children from play, lead them to seek work as the best of sports. This miracle few people will believe till they see it. The world is much more ready to accept past miracles than future.

But Montaigne is here as shrewd as ever in his observation. Children play with a worklike spirit, and indeed with them play is creative, aiding the growth of body and mind. For adults, games are utterly barren, and men with bats and cues and cards in their hands become children without the saving unconsciousness of childhood. A company of Englishmen on a lawn, spending their breath upon cricket, is no whit more respectable than a knot of Germans or Frenchmen in an *estaminet*, intent round a marble table upon a bout of dominoes. Both are excusable to that broad, unpriestly charity, that covers with the sweep of its unpaid absolution all delinquencies. You forgive them as you forgive the theft of a meal by a pauper. Under the goad of moral hunger they steal from Time and Labor, the trustful stewards of Nature and Art, the guardians and treasurers of humanity, twin partners of the Divine Architect and eternal prime Motor.

To its school Düsseldorf attracts some foreign artists, among them our countrymen, who get quickly on the scent of a good thing. A distinguished German painter told me, that of a number of young American painters whom he had known, not one was without talent, but that they did not study with due thoroughness. Structures of art to be good and durable, have as much need as cotton-factories of solid foundations. Genius can no more dispense with labor, than the eagle can with growth; the growth of genius is only through methodical application. The strokes of scientific work are the pulsations that carry nutriment to the genial germ, and make it accrescent. But genius discovers its own science, and finds often slow furtherance on the beaten roads of routine. American artists, with more boldness and freedom, carry to European academies a national impatience of delays, which may make some overleap the earlier indispensable gradations. But these are not the most gifted, for natural gifts feed themselves with the best food within their reach, as infallible in their selection as the roots of prosperous oaks. So far from being too self-reliant, genius has a quick faculty of absorbing and assimilating to itself the fruits of others' thoughts and practices. Plodding talent lags behind the pioneers and discoverers, nimble genius never. It fuses in its focal fire all things about it, so that, whether for beauty or for strength, they flow into the moulds it is fashioning.

In the studio of an American artist of high reputation in Germany as well as in America, I had one of those pleasant surprises that quicken the pulse more healthfully than a draft of old wine. On entering Leutze's spacious studio I came unexpectedly upon his fine picture of Washington crossing the Delaware. I had not heard that he was at work on such a picture. My heart was suddenly flooded with a sublime home-feeling. In Washington's majestic figure, the distant home, which he had done so much to build for me, became instantly present in a foreign land. What a bequest to his countrymen is this man's character. The great things he did are almost less than what he does. The image of him that grows into the mind of every young American, is a defence of his country as strong and steadfast now, a half-century since he died, as was in life his generalship and civil wisdom. His perpetual great presence is a national moral fortification.

Another artist who has not wrought with the pencil but with a deeper instrument, was this summer living at Düsseldorf, the Poet Freiligrath, who having dedicated his genius to the cause of German emancipation, had made himself a mark for the hate and persecution of a retrograde government.

CHAPTER XVI.

CLEANLINESS—BELGIAN PROSPERITY—STATISTICS.

PERFECT cleanliness were general perfection. A man whose body should be absolutely clean, always, without soil outwardly or inwardly, were a model man, a breathing ideal, what is often named but never seen—a perfect gentleman. Body and soul are so closely married, and so content with the bond, that strongest spiritualists and materialists, countertugging for centuries with combined might to sunder them, have not started a joint, but their interdependence and reciprocal benefactions continue unweakened, visible in all the myriad phenomena of life, their marriage being as indissoluble as that between man and woman, the which, under varying conditions, must ever be, growing freer and purer as we near the Utopia of perfect cleanliness.

But mutual dependence kills not freedom; nay, freedom is a product of mutual dependence. Thence, the body may be cleaner than the mind, and the reverse. The co-operation is not inflexibly uniform. I doubt whether the five thousand best scholars of Germany are bodily so clean, as the five thousand busiest bagmen of England. For every result there is always more than one cause. In the main, however, mental cleanliness precedes corporeal, here as elsewhere the moral element acting the masculine part, and taking the initiative.

The more animal men are, the less have they of personal cleanliness. Savages are dirtier than barbarians, whose habits again are not acceptable to educated civilizees. Ritual ablutions, like those of Mahometans, are not a full substitute for the washings that are consequent on culture. Communities or nations that are stagnant, are dirty. Movement purifies men as well as air. So soon as a man rises from lowness, and becomes progressive, he grows sweeter. The same with a people. Speaking of the practices of the Bretons in France, noted for their primitive ignorance, some one reported of them that they bring their pigs into their houses at night; "Oh! the dirty pigs," said Victor Hugo. The Brettons are supposed to be unmixed Celts, a variety of the white race not pre-eminent for cleanliness.

The English are the cleanest people of Europe, a distinction which is not shared with their fellow-subjects, Welsh, Scotch, or Irish. Next come the Dutch and Belgians, whose virtue on this side shines most, however, in their houses and streets, so that it is a satisfaction to cross from Germany or from France, into Belgium. To learn that the interior condition does not match with the outward, one has only to sojourn for a few weeks in a small Belgian town. But any advance in cleanliness is grateful and important, and a man who wears a fresh collar and bosom over a dirty shirt and an unwashed skin, is a better neighbor at table than if he had frankly exhibited his soiled linen. Nor is the Belgian neatness a false collar, it is genuine so far as it goes.

On coming into Belgium, the travellers who, witnessing the activity in Liege and in the docks of Antwerp, and beholding the spaded tillage of the fields, should talk only with the wealthy and read the *Indêpendance Belge*, or the *Emancipation*, might excusably follow the common error that the Belgians are a very prosperous people. While in 1848, their neighbors of Germany and France were in hot insurrection, they remained cool; they are thriving and happy, and have nothing to gain by change.

Over nations as over men, there is in our misorganized Christendom a thick crust of hypocrisy, under which, instead of the sweet juices of what is ripe and healthful, are crudities and putrescence. Let us break this crust, and note what we find beneath it in Belgium.

The official report* of the census, taken in 1848, makes known the number of families in Belgium to be 890,566, and of inhabitants 4,337,196, being about five persons to each family.

The habitations of these 890,566 families contain 2,758,966 rooms, including cellars and inhabited garrets, giving to each family three rooms. Little enough, and less than is needful for health or comfort, or even decency. But this is the average. Many families have more than three rooms, and many therefore less. The census declares that

154,454 families have each but one room;
282,785 families, each two;
453,327, three or more.

Thus 437,239 families, making almost one half of the Belgium nation, have each but one or two rooms for their whole habitation.

Over two millions of men, women, and children, every five of whom are lodged in one or two wretched rooms, badly lighted and worse ventilated, and in winter poorly warmed; this one room or two, serving as dining-room, kitchen, storeroom, cellar, work-room, sleeping-room, with rotting straw for beds, or leaves which you may see them gathering for this purpose in autumn, on the highway.

In the cities, the proportion of families that have but one or two rooms is larger than in the country. Antwerp counts 18,000 families, 11,000 of which have but one or two rooms. Brussels has 30,000 families, 13,700 of which have but a single room, and 6,800 two rooms. The medical commission of the city of Brussels, declares that the abodes of the greatest part of the laborers of

* See the speech of M. de Perceval, member of the Belgian Chamber of Representatives.

that city, are "living tombs whither these wretched men come to rest themselves, after twelve hours of work."

The food of these two millions is chiefly rye bread and potatoes, and a limited quantity of these. In "good times," they have meat or fish once or twice a week, but it is the refuse of the markets—liver, lungs, heart, intestines, what in America is given to dogs.

On the 30th of June, 1850, in the provinces of Flanders, out of a population of 1,415,484 there were 349,438 inscribed on the list of paupers.

The habitations of half the population of Belgium are hot-beds for the forcing of physical and moral evils. Diseases generated by bad air and bad diet sweep off annually thousands of puny children.

From these two millions what is to be looked for morally and intellectually for themselves, for the state. A man who has worked twelve hours to earn twenty cents, and then drags himself through the stenches of filthy alleys to the stale odors of a pestilential home, to find there a haggard toil-worn wife, and sad, pale, hungry children, a supper of coarse brown bread, and a bed of foul straw, what moral content, what civic strength do his slumbers replenish? He lies down without a thank for the day that is ended, he rises without a hope for the day that is beginning.

When two millions out of four and a half writhe in this unhuman degradation, the others will not have exemption from the ills of physical and moral poverty. The most favored of a community cannot so isolate themselves but that against them will react the condition of the lowest, through conductors which no strength or skill can cut. The chastest maiden, whose thoughts and sensations build round her a halo that draws the homage of the purest, cannot, on the highest social elevation, escape infection from the sickly breath of the harlot, whom she is yet too innocent to know of. It strikes like the inpalpable vapors of the pest. Unconsciously to herself her moral being is modified by the proximity of this social disease. Under Russian despotism, Belgian constitutional monarchism, American republicanism, men must form communities, they must have much in common, and cannot be rid of mutual dependence. In a higher social organization this dependence, which men now seek vainly to shake off, will be cultivated and a thousand-fold multiplied and strengthened, and with its strength will grow each man's moral and intellectual power and his freedom.

In a social or political whole, whether constructed on a sound or fragile basis, parts dovetail into parts, individuals into individuals. Connected, intermingled, interlaced with the two millions of semi-paupers of Belgium are other two millions of fellow-laborers, having more skill, many of them a little capital, earning instead of a franc, two, three, five francs, or more per day, who are most of them thus enabled to exchange often brown bread for white, and to garnish their potatoes and beans with more or less of animal nutriment. The iron hand of poverty is not on them, it is only suspended over their heads, and from them are replenished the ranks of the lowest masses, thousands annually slipping through the restless sieve of trading competition.

Of the 890,566 families not more than ninety thousand, if so many, are clear of the pressure of straitened means. Three or four hundred thousand individuals, out of four and a half millions, whose daily life is softened by the comforts of civilization, who along with spacious carpeted lodging, meats fatted and cooked with art, the luxuries as well as the utilities furnished from flax, cotton and wool, enjoy leisure for culture, exemption from over-work and the freedom of movement allowed by pecuniary ease. These favored few are the upper ranks of the "liberal professions," the bankers, merchants and large traders, the higher civil and military officers of the state, those who have inherited large capital, especially the "Noblesse," who, though now unrecognized by the state, enjoy with wealth the highest social position.

Relatively to the four millions below them, these four hundred thousand have a happy existence ; relatively to, not a hopeless ideal, but to a condition attainable within the limits of a generation by a hundred millions of living Christians, their life is barren, encumbered, slavish.

I have cited Belgium, not because its statistics present a peculiarly dark picture, but because, on the contrary, in Europe it is regarded as a shining model of national weal. Bad enough, that "Statesmanship" and Political Economy should bring nations to this pass ; worse, that they know not how to get them out of it ; worst, that they perceive not the need of getting them out of it.

CHAPTER XVII.

FRANCE—DEMOCRACY—BONAPARTE—LOUIS PHILIPPE—LOUIS BONAPARTE.

VIVE la République!

We have crossed the line that divides Belgium from France. Vive la République! What a promise, what a hope is in that shout! What achievements it proclaims, what consummations it prophesies! Not with the outward voice of a catching momentary fervor, bet solemnly from the depths of a soul-enkindled feeling be that stirring sound re-uttered. It is the rally-cry of Christendom. To France all Europe looks with hope. She is the centre of the new regenerating movement. Regenerating, not because it substitutes Presidents for Kings, citizen-representatives for Barons; but because it is to break down political monopoly, to make governors amenable to the governed, and, far more than this, because by giving each man a vote, it is to raise each voter to be a man.

Economy, simplicity, supplanting military by civil processes, less partiality in legislation and administration, wiser legislators and administrators (for this in the long run is the result), equality before the law, bettering of most public methods,—all these are the minor gains of republicanism, whose essential virtue is in the energizing of the primary elements, in the recognition, cultivation, refinement, enlargement of the substance out of which all forms of policy spring, and upon which they re-act, viz.: the masses of a nation, the individuals of its component multitudes, in Europe so brutified by monarchic and aristocratic despotism as to have been lately designated by a leading "Statesman," M. Thiers, as *la vile multitude*.

Democracy is the diffusion, and at the same time the invigoration of light and organic life. It vitalizes the remotest parts; through it, generic power permeates the whole social body. It is a substitution of man for the State, of men for things, of souls for bodies. Demanding liberty, it creates what it needs; it begets the vigor whereby it is to be braced. Proclaiming the power of self-government, it develops a broader, deeper self. He who believes not in self-government is less than a democrat; he who does is more. Democracy is progressive and expansive. Its ascendency is the gain of much liberty, and the assurance of more.

Honor to France. A glory greater than that dazzling one whereby she was so long blinded is hers, the glory due to boldness and insight in social transformations. In this sphere more fruitful will be her courage than in the battle-field, although on that there may be still some last laurels for her to gather. Napier, in his History of the Peninsular War, celebrating the brilliant bravery of a French charge, notes as a characteristic of French nature, that the first fiery onslaught being repelled, their line is disheartened. They lack elasticity under defeat. Not so in that other higher field. With fresh hope and spirit they have returned to the charge under the banner of Democracy, after lying for fifty years in defeat. And again partially worsted after the triumphant onslaught of 1848, they exhibit a determination, fortitude, calmness, forbearance, that bespeak convictions matured by thought, and a confidence that cannot be broken by discomfiture.

The morning of new eras is liable to be overcast; but blinded by ignorance or fear or malignity are they who mistake this transitory obscuration for a relapse to the past darkness. A people that has in it the juices for mature strength may be retarded in its progress, but not arrested ; and what seem forced retardations from without may be the natural currents of occult growth. The political revolutions of such a people can no more go back than can the planetary revolutions of the earth. Evolutions they should be called, for they are developments, however crashing may be the inaugurating acts. Democracy, or self-government, lies potentially at the heart of every people, that is, of every people of the white races. The time and manner of its emergence depend on mental constitution and outward influences. In England, where its spirit was ever strong, it took possession of the State under the Commonwealth, but it had not yet the cordial strength to impel itself arterially into all the members; and the most capable man whom it created being by nature despotic instead of generous, regal instead of Christian, principles were smothered under usurpations, so that the bastard monarchy of Cromwell was at his death easily supplanted by the legitimate monarchy of the Stuarts. Many too of the most resolute for freedom had already fled across the sea to the newly discovered Continent, there on its virgin shores, unbefouled by the tares of oligarchical egotism, to lay foundations whereon was to rise a political fabric of purely-democratic architecture, whose starry flag, unfurled at the end of the 18th century, was before the middle of the 19th to challenge the regards of the world as that of a preponderating Power among Christian States. Democracy had, if not its birth, its first wide national development in America.

In France it came forth a blind Samson, and buried itself under the ruins caused by its rageful grasp. Its movement was that of the loosened lion, whose courage is made frantic by hunger and fear. Men glared on men like unchained demons in a famished hell. With insane relish they lapped blood : that was their elixir for political renovation.*. But all this was transient, ex-

* In the massacre of St. Bartholomew, seventy thousand Frenchmen were slain, two thousand of them in Paris. During the two years of the

plosive phenomena, the agony of a great people's travail where nature had been poisoned, the convulsive writhings of an awakening giant against gyves and handcuffs. It denoted the great strength of the binding cords, and the still greater of the power that rent them. This power had at last recognized itself, and no bonds could ever again durably enthrall it. But here, as in England, the strongest child democracy had nursed, wielded the might wherewith she endowed him for the transitory ends of an impious ambition.

Bonaparte was behind his age; he was a man of the past. The value of the great modern instruments and the modern heart and growth he did not discern. He went groping in the mediæval times to find the lustreless sceptre of Charlemagne, and he saw not the paramount potency there now is in that of Faust. He was a great cannoneer, not a great builder. In the centre of Europe, from amidst the most advanced, scientific nation on earth, after nineteen centuries of Christianity, not to perceive that lead in the form of type is far more puissant than in the form of bullets; not to feel that for the head of the French nation to desire an imperial crown was as unmanly as it was disloyal, that a rivalry of rotten Austria and barbaric Russia was a despicable vanity; not to have yet learnt how much stronger ideas are than blows, principles than edicts—to be blind to all this, was to want vision, insight, wisdom. Bonaparte was not the original genius he has been vaunted; he was a vulgar copyist, and Alexander of Macedon, and Frederick of Prussia were his models. Force was his means, despotism his aim; war was his occupation, pomp his relaxation. For him the world was divided into two—his will, and those who opposed it. He acknowledged no duty, he respected no right, he flouted at integrity, he despised truth. He had no belief in man, no trust in God. In his wants he was ig-

"Reign of Terror," from '92 to '94, two thousand eight hundred and thirty-seven were executed in Paris.

noble, in his methods ignorant. He was possessed by the lust of isolated, irresponsible, boundless, heartless power, and he believed that he could found it with the sword and bind it with lies; and so, ere he began to grow old, what he had founded had already toppled, and what he had bound was loosed. He fell, and as if history would register his disgrace with a more instructive emphasis, he fell twice; and exhausted France, beleaguered by a million of armed foes, had to accept the restored imbecile Bourbons.

But that could not last a generation. For a dozen years the military boots of Napoleon had trodden down the crop of aspirations and thoughts that sprang up with the Revolution, but had not killed them. The soldier's heel cannot stamp the life out of ideas. They had lived and made roots in silence and secrecy, under the ghastly saturnalia of bloody fruitless conquests and Imperial tyrannies and ostentations. With the old men had come back the old egotisms, the old arrogances, the old inhumanities, the old feudal desires. But the old narrow forms had been shattered, the old growths cut up by the roots, and in their place were new wants, new hopes, new convictions. The old men, brought back by the enemies of France, stood isolated round the old throne. The nation was against them, and more than the nation, new truths were against them. Now was manifest the virtue of the great bloody revolution. It had engendered a new mind, broader, deeper, more earnest, higher, stronger, richer than the old one; and the young generation that entered the arena at the downfall of Napoleon, enlightened by its fire, exalted by its vigor, was the eager heir of the principles, without being contaminated by the errors, of the revolution. The propped throne was again upset, and the kingly brother of Louis XVI. was not, like him, brought to the block, but driven from France. In the "three days of July," 1830, the patchwork of the Holy Alliance was by the indignant people torn to shreds.

But a bulky old State, so deeply diseased, in order to be purged and righted, needs several crises. Its huge load of malady it can only be rid of through successive throes. France had yet to carry on her breast for some years, the imposthume of Royalty. The "Reign of Terror" was vivid in the memory of many, and its bloody image still rose up minatory whenever men directed their thoughts towards practical republicanism. The sins of that lurid epoch were not yet expiated. "Vive le Roi!" no longer a cordial cry, was still for a season to be the only one legal. Many even of the republicans accepted the project of "a throne surrounded by republican institutions." This absurdity had to be tried in order to be known. One would suppose, that the shapelessness of such a political monster would have been apparent to men's minds without the shock of practical evidence. Louis Philippe, the head of the younger branch of the Bourbons, was declared King.

This man's life, previously to his gaining the throne, was one long promise; his life on the throne, was one long lie. The bond for "republican institutions" was kept by restricting the right of voting at all to the election of the lower Chamber, and limiting the number of voters to the two hundred thousand richest men of France; by the creation of a House of Peers appointed by the King; by the most rigid centralization of all legislative and administrative power; by obstructing and gagging the Press, and withholding the right of meeting: by upholding, in so far as he could, the despotisms of Europe. Like all men who merely calculate, Louis Philippe miscalculated. In his own bosom he had naught wherewith to measure the moral force of mankind. Sordid and unscrupulous himself, he believed that all men could be bought, and that by buying a half million he could control the nation, and consolidate the throne for himself and his family. Himself and his family, this was his absorbing thought: self-aggrandizement was the end, France and Frenchmen were but his means. He was endured for eighteen long years, when France, betrayed and corrupted, wrathful at his want of faith, disgusted at his baseness, thrust him ignominiously from his perjured throne, giving him the remnant of his contemptible life to wear it out in England, where he died as he had lived, his mind teeming to the last with intrigues and hypocrisies.

Now swelled the popular heart. To claim their long sequestered rights, the millions came forth, strong in hope, strong in justice, strong with a new intelligence, strong in their forbearance, their forgiveness. The Republic was declared, and with it universal tolerance, and a many-sided freedom. But the goal of a stable liberty was not yet attained. The Royalists were routed, not annihilated. Too weak for open war, they had strength for secret mischief. The Republicans themselves were not united. Fresh convulsions ensanguined the streets of Paris, and embittered the public mind. Moreover, France had yet another expiation to make. She had to expiate the sin of pride in Napoleon and of the vanity of military glory. His spirit was to give her one more scourging. At her call, he came back in the emaciated shape of his nephew, elected through universal suffrage by an immense majority, the first President of the Republic.

Louis Bonaparte is cunning, resolute, and unscrupulous, with an ordinary intellect and an ordinary heart, and thence without principles or convictions. He is an ambitious mediocrity. His ambition being of that vulgarest kind, that springs from an intense love of self, is unleavened by any enthusiasm or expansiveness. He took the oath as President with Empire in his heart. That a man of this calibre should in the 19th century be in a position even to aspire to be Emperor of France! To gain the Imperial diadem, Napoleon did immense things; and repeated them, in order to wear it for a brief space. The largest thing the nephew will do in his lifetime, will be to have aspired to fill his uncle's seat. His dream will be his greatest deed. No spectacle is more pitiable than that of a small man in a great place. France, by offering this spectacle to the world in her first President, is expiating Napoleonism.

Napoleon, Louis Philippe, Louis Bonaparte,—here is an anti-climax of rulers. Rulers! Baffled bunglers. The day for the rule of men is passed. Even the strong Napoleon was incapable of ruling. The Christian world has outgrown individual rulers; ideas, principles now rule. He who in authority is not imbued, bemastered by these, is at most an obstruction that temporarily angers the current, which, arrested for a time, chafes and eddies, and then sweeps into the abyss all that obstructs it. The great Bonaparte was so swept down; and the wary Louis Philippe; yet now, when the stream is far deeper and stronger, the little Bonaparte would thrust forward his petty personality to divert its flooding course, to make its boiling waters back! The highest that a shrewd judgment could have devised for such as he is, had been, to float for a season the apparent helm of the State, on the ocean of Democracy.

For, Democracy, with the broad deep principles which it involves and unfolds, is henceforward to rule in France. Ideas, once rooted in a great people, cannot be uptorn. They grow until they embrace with their life every being on the soil. With their wide sun-like warmth they grasp the cold egotisms of a departed power, that vanish before them like icicles before the solstitial rays.

Over the portal of the Palace, where this soulless retrospective aspirant would already play the mimic Emperor, are largely stamped words that are to him, and to all who with him or like him plot for regal or imperial sway, a terrific writing on the wall: Liberty, Equality, Fraternity. Before these great words, illuminated by a nation's faith, they recoil stricken with dread, so committed are they to usurpation, so tethered to fraud and force, so blinded by sensuality, so hateful of what is noble and generous.

These sublime words, uttered in a mood of prophetic exaltation, proclaim the beauty and unsounded potency of the human heart. These beautiful words, the tokens of things more beautiful, re-assert the Christian promise of love and peace. They are a rainbow splendor, painted on the evanescent clouds of despair by the eternal Sun of hope.*

* Since this chapter was written has come the *coup d'état* of Louis Bonaparte. This usurpation seems to dash the hopes and confound the estimates herein expressed. If the life of a nation were reckoned by months and years and not by decades and centuries, it would do so. A great Christian people cannot go back. Principles must triumph over expedients. I believe in God, not in the Devil; in the victory of good over evil.

CHAPTER XVIII.

A DAY IN PARIS.

At six in the morning of May 20th, 1851, through the tall, wide chamber-window, that lets in light from ceiling to floor, my just-awakened eyes look from my pillow upon the green plane-trees that grow in the vacant lot opposite to No. 8 *rue du Helder*. Their large foliage is shaking coolly in the morning breeze. In the centre of Paris this tree-decked void is now rare. Favored is the Parisian lodger who has such opposite neighbors. They adorn my room, and make me free in it: they are at once my curtains and my companions.

The hour of waking is a solemn hour. We have just past suddenly from darkness into light, from death to life. Unconscious babes we come crying into the world, and this matinal re-birth is a conscious daily entrance upon a scene of sorrow. It is the hour when yesterday is nearest,—yesterday that silently wrings the conscience, like the saddened gaze of a dying friend whom we have wronged. He is gone forever, and we have not been to him what we should have been. But we get hardened to these retrospective upbraidings, and thrusting yesterday behind us in thought as he is in fact, we turn in our bed,—the will not being yet enough electrified to lift us out of recumbency into uprightness,—and boldly or timorously, despondently or hopefully, indifferently or cheerfully, we confront the new day that the sun has just brought to us from the mysterious East. For myself, being bent on extra work, action cuts short meditation, and I leap out of bed into water at 58° Fahrenheit,—a temperature to be recommended to those who possess the privilege of beginning every day with a cold bath.

The window unlatched, turning on double hinges like a folding door, opens its whole expanse. Fresh and sweet the morning air rolls in, untainted up here in the *Premier* (what we should call the third story) by the impurities of the pavement. The cries of Paris are in full chorus, the old-clothes men leading the peripatetic band. Opposite, a hydrant,—set running for two hours morning, noon and evening for domestic service and to gargle the gutters,—pours forth a vigorous stream, that seems to delight in its own cool gush.

—— Issuing through the *porte-cochère* into the street, a little past seven, a few steps bring us to the corner, where we surprise the *Boulevard des Italiens* in complete deshabillé. Brooms, dusters, water-pails are busy; shop-windows are disgarnished; cafés are turned out of doors to be swept; the broad sidewalks, the afternoon home for swarms of idlers, are unpeopled, save by the initiatory providers of the day, the indispensable purveyors, who could be as ill spared as the Sun with whom they rise, the bread-men and water-men and milk-men. Sad-looking women are on their way to the close hives, where a whole day's lung-and-eye-wearing stitchwork earns for them a minimum of life's first necessaries. An ice-cart, with its circular thatched roof, is at Tortoni's.—We have reached the *Boulevard Montmartre;* the shade on the east side is already welcome. Opposite, a line of cabs, mostly of royal blue with white ponies, has taken its stand of passive expectancy. Cabmen are favored: they enjoy several of the first elements of well-being. They are all day in the open air; they are never like other mortals deserted by hope, upon which it may be said they chiefly live; they frequent the best houses, keep good company, and always ride. In return for these blessings, they are contented and civil; and if, to their small perquisite you add a *sous* or two, they on their part will add to their "merci, monsieur," a cordiality and gratitude of tone that at once make you the gainer by the gift.

The daily inaugurating act of each house in Paris is, to purge itself of the sweepings and rejected kitchen-fragments of the past twenty-four hours, which are thrown out in piles on the edge of the sidewalk, where they await the scavenger-carts that come along towards eight. But ere these can arrive squalid Poverty, pricked out of sleep by Hunger, has started from its filthy couch, and dispersed through the streets its tattered hordes. At this moment over every pile of garbage bends a hungry proletarian, seeking therein his breakfast, and it may be his dinner. Look at that man, a deep, wide-mouthed basket strapped to his back. With a short stick, hooked at one end, he rakes into the pile, drives his hook into rag or paper, delivers what he has pinned into the basket, with a rapid jerk of the stick over his shoulder, and ferrets again into the foul heap with an eye made keen by want. Here is another who has laid down the hook, and with his hands is picking out bones. I have seen a man and a dog fraternally exploring the same pile. A little further a woman is sorting, at the edge of the gutter, the rejected lemon-peels of a *café;* the best of them,—for to poverty there is choice in lowest degrees,—she throws into her basket, and will perhaps, out of this refuse of an orgie, concoct a savory draft for her sick child. These are the *chiffoniers*, the rag-gatherers.

Seizing a moment of intermittence in the flow of carts, man-drawn as well as horse-drawn, and of lazy-looking cabs, we cross the *rue Montmartre*, one of the great arteries of Paris. We meet squads of laborers in blue *blouses*, with tools on shoulder, going to their work, distant for many of them a league or more from their homes in the *quartier St. Antoine*,—if homes those can be called where there is so little of privacy and comfort for the few hours they are in them. On the edge of the sidewalk of the *Boulevard Bonne Nouvelle* three drivers of public sprinkling-carts are lying, two of them asleep. Through the band of the broad-brimmed drab hat of each is a rosebud, shining on that coarse ground, like Beauty guarding the slumbers of Strength.

We are now at the *Porte St. Denis.* The mile that we have come on the *Boulevard* is but a small segment of this longest, broadest, freest, most commodious, most lively, most variegated, most magnificent of urban avenues in the world. The width of this queen of streets is about one hundred and thirty feet, the one half in asphalte sidewalks. The *Porte St. Denis* is a triumphal arch seventy feet high, erected more than a century since on the foundations of one of the old gates of Paris in honor of the victorious campaigns of Louis XIV. On the entablature you read in large capitals, LUDOVICO MAGNO. Monumental inscriptions that are not rescripts of the general judgment are speechless. Emphasize, begild, emblazon them as you will, they have no voice. A score of triumphal arches could not make *great* stick to Louis XIV., and this *Magno* is but an impotent ostentation.

As we retrace our steps, the Boulevard is fuller. Here a flower-woman has just taken her stand. For a bunch of rosebuds she asks ten cents and takes eight, and would probably have taken six. She is a type of all traders, great and small, whose aims, means, and whole practice may be codified into one brief precept;—buy as cheap and sell as dear as you can.—For a moment our passage is obstructed by a herd of she-asses who, with their habitual countenance of grave resignation, are coming up to the door of an invalid, to whom ass's milk has been prescribed by some doubting, dogmatic doctor. The stream of busy humanity that pours out of the *Passage Jouffroy* towards the heart of the city, deepens. Some are reading, as they walk, the morning papers, which they have just bought at a news-stall. It is nearly eight when we re-enter the gate of the *Hotel du Tibre.*

—— This is the hour for breakfast and the newspapers, both excellent; for the bread and the butter of Paris are sweet, and the newspapers are the most readable in the world. A virtue of French nature is, that it is intolerant of a bore. With Frenchmen the *style ennuieux* is the only bad style. Their best pens work for the newspapers. At this moment a score of the cleverest members of the National Assembly are habitual contributors to them. Novelists, poets, men of science, critics of high name, fill daily their *feuilletons*. The Paris journals have less quantity and finer quality, less matter and more spirit, less about trade and more about taste, than those of England or America.

The French speakers and writers are sounding the depths of politics with as much ability as boldness. Their expositions throw fresh light on our practice. From several of the most marked of the Paris journals of this morning I will take a few sentences as samples of the political opinions and hopes of the day.

The *Assemblée Nationale*,—said to be under the influence of M. Guizot,—shall speak in a single sentence for all the Royalists :—" Oui, puisque la République est une nécessité du temps, de la confusion des idées et de l'abaissement des courages, subissons la avec résignation." The resignation here preached means resistance at the first opportunity; for the Royalists have understanding and will not understand, and they do sincerely believe that when they shall have gotten rid of Louis Bonaparte, they can permanently put down democracy. As wisely employed would they be in trying to put down light. Is the Sun too luminous for them, they can in no other way escape his rays than by retreating from the upper earth into cellars and caverns. Can they not bear the fertilizing heat of Democracy, let them withdraw into the wildernesses of Asiatic despotism. Europe is no place for them. For Europe, under the momentum imparted by Christianity, thought, science, instinct, is galloping into democracy.

It might be thought, that the Thiers and the Guizots, and the Broughams, being shrewd, practised men, know better, and are hypocrites when they denounce Democracy. To account for their proceeding, their sincerity need not be questioned. The intellectual vision of such men gets obscured by egotism. They commenced as light-dispensing liberals, but having within them no cordial love of truth to keep their minds warm and elastic, they have become narrowed and petrified by conceit and ambition. They never were other than political adventurers, self-seeking speculators in the market of Politics.

The *Pays* has lately come under the control of Lamartine. Writing to-day on the "Republic which best suits France," he combats the project of an Executive named by the Assembly. Here is a brick from his pile :—"Une Assemblée exécutant elle-même, sans division des pouvoirs, c'est la confusion des pouvoirs, c'est l'irrésponsabilité du gouvernment, c'est l'impunité de toutes les oppressions contre le peuple, c'est la tyrannie à mille têtes! C'est la Convention! En voulez vous?"

The *République*, in an article headed, "Monarchie ou République," and signed *Ad. Guéroult*, says:—"Il s'agit de choisir entre le régime paternel de l'Autriche et le gouvernement du pays par lui-même; de retourner au moyen-age, on du continuer la Révolution Française. Qui pourra douter du résultat?"

The *Presse*, when its proprietor, Emile de Girardin, puts his soul into it as he does just now, is the ablest journal in Christendom. It glows this morning with power. By its zeal, ability and vigor, it is the most efficient expounder of the great democratic movement in France and Europe.

To royalist papers, quarrelling about the elder and younger branches of the Bourbons, M. de Girardin says:—"Ne vous querellez pas: ni les cadets ni les ainés de la maison de Bourbon ne reviendront en France, à moins qu'il ne leur convienne d'y revenir sans autre prétension que celle de simples citoyens, électeurs et éligibles.

"Le droit commun est devenu le droit absolu ; il n'admet pas d'exceptions.

"Les Monarchistes ont tué la Monarchie en France : les fusionistes l'ont enterrée."

—— The limitations of time and space, the inexorable conditions to which he is subjected by his body and his watch pinch the stranger, who wishes to crowd into one Paris day a great variety of objects and sensations. He must hurry and be content with glimpses. But the deathless mind has no such limitations. In a second it sweeps through æons, or embraces the orbits of siderial systems. Within the compass of a few minutes, while you are passing through a Church or a Museum, long chapters of thought can write themselves upon the brain. I shall not so abuse the indulgence of the reader, who permits me to lead him about the Capital of France, as to transcribe the half of this writing. Were I to do so, instead of an hour,—he would need a day to read "a day in Paris." I spare him.

Among the cardinal objects of Paris, one of the nearest to our lodgings is the National Library, in the *rue Richelieu*, the largest in the world, containing more than a million of volumes. We arrive just as the guardians are throwing open its immense galleries at ten.

A vast compact collection of books is a table of contents of the world past and present, an epitome of human kind up to the living hour. What our predecessors on the globe have thought and done is here registered. Manuscripts, Syriac, Coptic, Arabic, fill any chasms that the briarean printing-press has not yet bridged over. From these shelves, men and nations speak and tell their story. Around you is a chronicle of your race. Those tribes whose nature and speech were too feeble to utter themselves in books, have been reported by their stronger kin.

Books denote intellectual wants satisfied; they are clasps wrought by culture to strengthen itself; they are testimonials of national character; they measure the degree of human vitality in a people. Those who have the best books will be found to be at the top of the scale, those who have none at the bottom. Recall the history of Nations, and survey a present map of the globe. Books are grains of spiritual wheat; I mean good books, such as have the life of fresh honest thought in them. A good library is a granary of thoughts; it stores up aliment for the mind; it preserves seed from all ages and countries, and, like the wheat discovered in the tombs of Egypt, this seed keeps its life for thousands of years, and if planted fructifies.

The sowing is here done broadcast, for in going the round of these gigantic halls we come upon one where, at a long table, sit a multitude of silent readers. Whoever wishes a book writes its name on a slip of paper. This the Librarian hands to one of his assistants, who perhaps has to walk through a furlong of books to fetch it. The volumes delivered to him the applicant must use in the library; he is not permitted to take them away.

Like a patriarch amidst his progeny, in the centre of one of the great halls, sits in permanent presidence, Voltaire,—Voltaire the skeptical, the witty, the versatile, the voluminous. The statue is a copy in plaster bronzed of that marvel of portrait-sculpture in the *Théatre Français*, by Houdon. The aged face sparkles with shrewdness. It is the head and face not of the wisest but of the most knowing of men. The countenance is that as of a man who had never wept. But in this it wrongs Voltaire: he was not without sympathy and kindliness. Nor was he, like Talleyrand, a man who believed in nothing but himself, and in his best moments doubted even that. Priests, whom his reason unmasked and his wit lashed, have done their worst to blacken Voltaire. With priests,—who live by creeds and credulity,—the direst offence is skepticism. But skepticism is never an original disease; it is a reaction against hypocrisy and false belief. Skepticism is the forerunner of a better belief, for men are by nature believers, and doubts are the braces of faith. The man who has never doubted is apt to be a shallow believer. To the generation that doubted with Voltaire has succeeded a generation, which, strengthened by the antecedent purgation through doubt, now believes with Béranger and with Lammenais, and with him who is the deepest and broadest believer and the most far-seeing man of his country and age, with Fourier, who came to harmonize the heart of man with the thought of God.

—— Turning to the left as we issue into the *rue Richelieu*, through the massive black portal of the Library, we soon cross the *rue neuve des Petits Champs*, and in a few paces come upon a short *passage*, by help of which, after descending a flight of stone steps, we suddenly find ourselves under an arched, open corridor, that encloses an oblong quadrangle, seven hundred feet by three hundred, planted with rows of truncated lime-trees, with grass-plots and flower-beds, fountains and statues in the centre. All round this immense corridor of two thousand feet are shops, and above it is one immense edifice, internally partitioned, horizontally as well as vertically, into hundreds of tenements, and is externally of uniform and florid architecture, with fluted pilasters and Corinthian capitals, and elaborate details of ornament. This is the *Palais Royal*, a compendium of the great Capital in whose midst it stands—a mammoth warehouse of the necessaries and the luxuries, the solids and the prettinesses, the grossnesses and the refinements of civilization. Here you may equip yourself for a journey or a ball; furnish a house or a trunk; fill your library or your larder; pass from the taciturn reading-room to the chattering *Estaminet*, to quicken time's pace by a game of billiards with *Charles* or *Romain;* wash down a twenty franc dinner with a bottle of *Clos Vougeot* at the *Trois Frères*, or a two franc one with thin *Bordeaux* at *Richard's* hard by; mount into the altitudes of Art with *Rachel*, or have *Levassor* help you digest your dinner with his side-shaking fun.

At this hour and season the spring-green leaves of the dwarfed lime-trees, which contrast harmoniously with their clean black branches, waste on the smooth gravel their rectilinear shade, not yet prized by the gossipping nurses, and less by the children that run among the legs of elderly loungers, who come to this sprightly seclusion, this palatial patch of French *rus in urbe*, to let indolence float them an hour or two down Time's lethean stream.

Besides the wealthy idle, there are in Paris thousands of people who, on incomes of from two hundred to five hundred dollars, lead a life of absolute unproductiveness. To this class, time is all pastime. Their meals are their occupations. For their attic lodgings, and other scant indispensables, they grudgingly pay their few francs daily. This is all they give; they are takers, not givers. They live on the community; that is, on what is common and open to all, which in Paris is so lively and various, that to the vacant it is as good as a fat property. In good weather they haunt the *Boulevards* and public gardens and gratis spectacles; in bad, the *cafés*, *estaminets*, auctions, passages, bazaars. Their personal relations are few. The responsibilities fed by the affections, the duties of worker, citizen, and friend, from these they emancipate themselves as fully as may be, in order to reduce existence to the minimum of care. This they call freedom, and in sadness we allow, that they are not wholly wrong; for under the civilized *régime*, such falseness is there in all relations, that he who has the fewest is the freest. What a freedom! obtained by personal isolation and moral micrification.

—— In five minutes we alight at the Church of *St. Germain l'Auxerrois*. This church has a dismal celebrity. From its belfry it was that on the 23d of August, 1572, was given the signal for the massacre of St. Bartholomew, and all through that awful night its bell tolled. Was it in penitence, or in triumph? The

Romish Church professes to be unchangeable. Are its priests then ready to re-commit that crime for which earth has no name? Did the executioners of that sacerdotal sentence afterwards bring their doings of that night to the confessional? Was the fulness of the absolution and its unction in proportion to the number of victims reported? Good God! that these godless impostors should still thrive! that men who have had opportunities and culture, men even of manly natures, should still submit themselves, their feelings and their acts, to the revision of this histrionic corporation!—But we will not stop longer on the threshold, to be embittered by the terrific retrospection, and the angry thoughts it awakens.

Within, two funeral services are going on; one in the middle of the church for a child, the other in a side chapel for an adult, and, from the tranquil acquiescent mien of the mourners, apparently, aged person. But from the group in the centre are heard the sobs of that sharp grief which cuts into the heart of the mother, and makes there a wound that never fully heals. Violence has been done, hence life-quaking sorrow; for early death, or death from any cause but decay, is against the normal law of nature. The painless death of the aged from exhaustion is the only natural death—painless to the departed, and painless, though sad, to the survivors.

In another recess an elderly priest is teaching the catechism to a large class of boys. French children in the earliest years are mostly not beautiful; they want the unconscious, untainted, selfless look, which, with a rosy transparent plumpness, makes cherubs of their little neighbors across the Channel; but among these boys, who were from ten to fourteen, there was much beauty. As we paused for a moment, the priest asked one of them to explain the mystery of the incarnation! The boy made answer according to the words of the book.

In a populous city like Paris, where there are few churches, and where so many thousands seldom visit them, except for the great sacraments, it were quite possible to hit upon an hour when, besides a funeral, there should be a marriage and a christening. As we had not this fortune, I almost regretted not to possess the gift that some reporters have, of eking out with inventions the short-comings of reality. Yet it was fitting that for this church, the image of death should stand alone in the memory.

—— Coming out, we front the east façade of the Louvre, and on the globe we could not stand on a spot from which to behold a grander architectural mass. A colonnade nearly two hundred yards long, of coupled Corinthian columns, each one thirty-eight feet high, supported on a plain basement thirty feet high, with a gallery behind pierced with windows and enriched with pilasters and festoons. But here, as in all great architectural creations, the enduring grandeur and beauty spring from the proportions. Were the basement a few feet lower, or the pairs of columns further apart, or the entablature less massive, or the central and lateral projections more prominent, the harmony would be broken, and this unique façade would have missed much of its renown. Possibly some of the details might be improved. The arching of the windows in the basement, the want of elevation in those above, the unmeaningness of the festoons over each upper window, if these are defects,—which I hardly presume to say they are,—they are merged in the splendor of effect produced by excellence of proportion among such gigantic constituents.

Those great Greeks! what a plastic genius, what a clear soul for beauty, what an infallible inward sense of form they had. Look at a Corinthian column, with its wrought base, its light fluted shaft, springing with a graceful strength up to its acanthine capital, like an elastic Flora bearing a basket of flowers above her head,—what a creation it is! Imperishable from its beauty, it is an ornament to the earth forever.

—— The Quays are one of the great features of Paris. Herein

she high overrides her mightier English rival. Ten miles of quay,—five on each side of the river,—of from fifty to eighty feet wide, paved, lighted, fenced by stone balustrades, one endless terrace overlooking the Seine, the one side communicating with the other by a dozen bridges,—it is a magnificence traversing the city, such as no other city in the world can show.

Ascending the quays on the right bank of the river, we cross the *Pont Neuf* to the island, where is the original city, the primary centre, round which by successive radiations has grown in the course of more than a dozen centuries, this vast metropolis. Passing by the *Palais de Justice*, we alight in front of the huge truncated towers of *Notre Dame*, the foundations of which were laid more than eight hundred years ago.

Seldom is there in architecture a transmission of life from part to part, a quick circulation of vitality through the members, melting them into a whole. The great law of unity, predominant and transparent in every work of Nature, and therefore imperative in Art, is from weakness seldom fulfilled in its severity. Now the imposing front of the famous old Cathedral of *Notre Dame*, is not enough penetrated by this unifying essence. The parts lie one above the other strata-wise. It cannot be called heavy, yet it presses too much on the earth. The best architecture is always buoyant, lifting itself up with an intrinsic nervousness, a self-sustainment, infused by beauty; for beauty has the virtue to spiritualize the bulkiest mass.

And the exterior is the best of it. The interior is in its *ensemble* less inspired. Those stout columns, besides being not Gothic, are grossly prosaic. Instead of mounting up with alacrity to meet the down-stooped roof, and carrying it without sign of effort, they look overladen, and as though they complained of their task. But here in the transepts is a compensating pomp, two circular painted windows, opposite the one to the other, and each fifty feet in diameter. They are like the magnification of a brilliant kaleidoscope.

These Gothic cathedrals are sublime efforts made in the middle ages, to embrace God with the uplifted arms of mighty Architecture.

—— Crossing over to the left bank of the river, we traverse part of the *quartier Latin* to reach the Luxembourg. We have time but for a short turn in its spacious, shady, hospitable garden, from which we hasten up to the gallery of living French painters.

With ever new zest one re-beholds that great picture of Couture, *Les Romains de la Décadence.* A capital excellence of this masterpiece is, that it illustrates and demonstrates the limitation of the Arts. Each art has its domain within which it is sovereign, beyond which it is uncrowned. Never did artist plant himself more firmly in the very centre of his rightful dominion than does Couture in this picture. Written poetry, sculpture, music, could not with their utmost attainment, singly or united, impress upon the mind an image of the decline of Rome, so vivid, so full, so convincing, as is here done on canvass in a single view.—A Roman orgie, in a lofty banquet-hall of cool Grecian architecture; men and women reclining, standing, sitting, some with goblets in hand; and over all the languor of an irremediable satiety. In that large, graceful, recumbent, central, female figure, what fallen majesty, what spent power, what a gigantic lassitude! in those big dark orbs what a depth of fixed sadness! Never more can that countenance beam with joy. Here a male figure has climbed up to a niche and offers wine to a statue; what a fine stroke of Art to express utter satiation. On the opposite side, a woman is tearing her hair, as if suddenly seized with madness, and nobody heeds her. In the distant background, a group are tearing one another. Here there is a show of dalliance, but lacking the sting of passion. In the love there is no fire, no flavor in the wine, nor in the grapes any slaking coolness. Palate and feeling, body and soul, all is *blasé,* consumed by a heat which warms not. Those two spectators in the corner, standing indignant, like Brutus and Cassius come back, they frown in vain. Mighty Rome is fallen forever. The Latin civilization is drained to the bottom, and here are the putrid lees. It had not the soul of the highest life. The spiritual element, the higher human, the vivacious and immortal, mingled in it too feebly to project it towards an indefinite progression. Its great animal intellectual vigor, has compassed the widest orbit yet permitted to a nation. Force has run its full circle, beginning in rude strength, and ending, naturally, in voluptuousness.

But already, as Rome passed her zenith, in the East had been laid the foundations of a power, on whose immeasurable path was to be borne, not a nation, but a host of nations, and not nations merely, but better than nations, MAN. Civilized Paganism was the consecration of the State; Christianity is the consecration of man. In Greece and Rome man was subordinated to the State; the more the law of Christ is fulfilled, the more the State is subordinated to man. The greater the concentration and exercise of power in the State, the smaller is man. When the State is all and man nothing, as under Despotism, the instrument rules its maker, and belittles him; for the State is of man, and man is of God. When Christianity grows strong, it strengthens man, and melts the bonds of the State. The freest nation must be the most Christian. The most unchristian power in Christendom is the Papacy.

The thoughts kindled by this great picture carry us away from the picture itself. Considering the almost unique felicity of the subject, the breadth of its purport, the intellectual beauty of its composition, the masterly richness of the execution, the high unconscious moral there is in it, this picture should rank as one of the greatest works of art in Europe. It is a canvas-compendium of Roman history. Study it, and save yourself the trouble of reading Gibbon.

—— The sun has passed the meridian, and will soon be hurrying away from us: we must hasten after him.—Coachman, drive as fast as safety and the police will let you. From the narrow, damp streets of this side the river, one issues upon the quays with a feeling of disenthralment. Turning to the left we descend the left bank. In view on the opposite shore are, the Louvre, its long gallery, the Palace, the garden of the Tuileries. On this side we drive along, first the learned quays Malaquais and Voltaire, with their book-stalls and print-shops, and the house where Voltaire died, then the Quay D'Orsay, with its imposing edifices and patrician tranquillity. Now are we crossing the *Pont de la Concorde*, from which the eye ranges up the river to be stopped two miles off by the towers of *Notre Dame*, and down, by distant foliage, then across to the *Place de la Concorde*, with its neighboring grandeurs. Flanked on the right by the massy foliage of the Tuileries, and on the left by *Elyséean* vistas under broken shade; with its two pompous fountains spouting their large expanse of clear, noisy water, between them the Obelisk of Luxor, looking in its solemn singleness like a mourner at a wedding; with its gay, bronze-gilt lamp-columns and bold statuary and incessant roll and glitter of carriages, and its magnificent environment, the *Place de la Concorde*, on every sunny day like this, wears a festal air. Now we are close upon the *Madeleine*, belted by more than fifty Corinthian columns, each one fifty feet high. For months this architectural paragon has been to me a daily joy; for, not a day but I pass it more than once, and never without fresh admiration and thankfulness. I will presume upon the privilege of having gazed at it many hundred times to find one fault in it. The pediment is not purely Grecian, but somewhat Roman, that is, a little too high. Were there a mile up the Boulevards a large specimen of pure Gothic, what termini there were to the gayest walk in Europe.

We reach the *rue du Helder* at one, most grateful for an hour's rest, which is made more refreshing by help of a mutton-chop and French roll for lunch.

—— It is half-past two when I find myself again on the other side of the river, and alighting at the corner of the Quay Voltaire, I walk into the *rue de Beaune*. No. 2 is the first gate-way on the right, entering the which I cross a broad court, ascend a few steps to the large open portal, turn to the right, and having passed through two doors in succession, have before me in a spacious, shelf-furnished room, several clerks, silently at work behind the wire netting that in French offices separates the visitor from the inmates. Invading this precinct, with interchange of salutation with the occupants, I issue out at the opposite angle, and traversing a short, dark passage, enter by a small door another capacious room with tall windows to the ground looking on a garden. At an enormous oval table in the middle of the room, covered with green baize and bestrown with newspapers, two bearded men are writing, and another is reading a journal, a sofa on one side is possessed in its full length by a recumbent fourth, while two or three others, seated before the coal embers of the large fire-place, are smoking short clay pipes. Conversation is fitful, now and then rising for a few moments into earnest continuity. This is the *sanctum* of the writers for the *Democracie Pacifique*, and the rendezvous of the Phalansterians. On the mantel-piece is a bust of Fourier.

These men believe in a new social order, to be founded on absolute justice; and they have dedicated themselves to the exposition of the laws whereby it is to be organized. Convictions of the present possibility of a more human and a more divine condition for man, contrasted with which the best he has yet had is but vanity and blight, these are the staple of their life. They live in a future, built of ideas originated by thoughtful, sympathizing genius. They themselves are not raised above their fellows by brilliancy of parts or purity of conduct; their distinction is, that, whether by the fortune of association, or by intellectual sympathy, or by æsthetic susceptibility, they have accepted the discoveries of Fourier. Providence provides that the good seed which she generates shall some of it light on soil where it can grow and fructify. They are not high on the social scale, but from the eminence of new truth they look calmly down upon the turmoil which men now call society. In the world's goods they are poor, but the incommensurable wealth of world-moulding ideas is theirs; and thus enriched, they already enjoy an inward well-being, which to flaunting grandees and bedizened officials, who think they despise them, were an incredible Utopia.

The bust of Fourier is unhappily not faithful. The artist has had the imbecile arrogance to alter God's work: he thought to improve it! He has "idealized" by squaring, enlarging, emboldening it; that is, he has annihilated Fourier, and instead of a transcript from the original head, he has given us a big, hollow, no-head. But the disciples of Fourier possess a cast from his cranium after death. This indicates a nature more distinguished for the completeness and harmony of its organization, than for any one-sided intellectual or affective superiority. I gazed at it as I had at his simple tomb in the cemetery of Montmartre, with deep emotion; for to this man I acknowledge myself to be under unspeakable obligations. He has ratified and enlightened my best intuitions; he has intellectualized my aspirations into scientific truths. His discoveries and deductions are new revelations of the greatness and goodness of God, and of the cognate power and splendor of man. "Les attractions sont proportionelles aux destinées;"—"La Série distribue les harmonies."* These two sublime formulas, into which Fourier has condensed the essence of his doctrine, and which prefigure the

* Attractions are proportionate to destinies;—the Series distributes the harmonies.

coming glorified condition of humanity, are as yet to the multitude cabalistic and enigmatical, and to the Pharisees what were, and continue to be to them the words of Jesus, " Love thy neighbor as thyself,"—" Be ye perfect, even as your Father which is in Heaven is perfect;" the which sublime exhortations are still an ideal goal, shining with a star-like brilliancy, and a star-like remoteness, through the night of human enmities and imperfections. The formulas of Fourier are the vehicle wherein this high ideal shall descend to the earth, and become the reality of daily life.

—— Re-crossing the Seine by the *Pont National,* I enter the Tuileries Gardens. Trees and turf are freshly robed in the clear, clean verdure of spring. On coming into these gardens one gains a sense of freedom. The sudden salutation of Nature in mid-urban closeness were enough for this, and Art enlarges the sensation by beautifying the welcome of Nature with her own graceful courtesy. With the leaves and flower-buds children have come back. The broad alley on the *rue Rivoli* is glittering with these soul-buds, and through the joyous, busy swarm one moves slowly, imbibing spiritual peace from celestial emanations.

Quitting the Garden by the gate opposite the arch-flanked *rue Castiliogne,* in five minutes I am in the *rue Duphot,* which ascends from that of *St. Honoré* to the *Boulevard des Capucines.* At No. 12 I pass under a solid gateway over which is inscribed, *Ecole d'Equitation,* where besides the best schooling in horsemanship in a spacious covered quadrangle, good well-equipt saddle-horses are to be had by the month or day. In a few minutes I have under me a clean-limbed English blood mare, in full trot up the broad avenue of the *Champs Elysées.* A ride on a mettled horse who enjoys his own springy motion, is a cure for many of the minor ills of life.

The sight cannot escape the gigantic Triumphal Arch which

crowns the eminence at the head of this noble avenue,—by far the most massive specimen in Europe of a vain and arrogant class of edifice, and a sample of the handiwork of Napoleon, who was so great in the smaller, the material sublime, and so small in the greater, the moral sublime. Two centuries hence this monument of military achievements will by the thoughtful of that period be interpreted as a naif record,—elaborately chiselled upon the tablet of History by the "Great Captain of the age,"—of the semi-barbarism of the nineteenth century, whereof himself was the most shining exemplification.

Leaving this monster* on the right, I join the current which, on the cushioned seats of coach or saddle, sets at this hour up the avenue of St. Cloud towards the *Bois de Boulogne.* This sandy area, about seven miles in circuit, covered for the most part by a stunted growth, chiefly of oaks and birch, is intersected throughout by numerous straight avenues that run across from edge to edge and cut one another at all angles. There is but one meandering path, running through the middle, and much frequented by equestrians. This is a pleasure-ground for that portion of Parisian idlers who can afford the daily luxury of horses. On Sundays all the hackney-carriages of Paris are in request to transport thither a fraction of the *Bourgeoisie.* But even hacks are beyond the reach of the mechanical and other hard-working classes. Those on whose broad, steadfast labor Society rests as her foundation, she dooms to exclusion even from the meagre relaxations which in her penury she doles out. In her diabolic perversity she honors most the least creative, those who consume much and produce nothing.

Here comes, on a stout sleek horse, a stout well-tailored man, with groom to match. His square fleshy face is sallow, his eye egotistic and unhappy. He looks like a rich sensualist hopelessly

* It cost two millions of dollars. For his own magnification, the Corsican spent the gold of Frenchmen as lightly as their blood.

riding for an appetite. In passing, he scans me, as though by my look he would measure my worldly importance. In a button-hole of his coat he has a red ribbon, and on his overcoat the same. Medals round the necks of children are hateful to me. They are mostly a falsehood, as not expressing the absolute relative merits of the wearers to their mates. They are often a testimonial of only apparent excellence; they are always a bait to draw vanity to the surface, and are therefore stimulants of a morbid emulation. They demoralize the child. On an adult they are disgusting, a stain on his manhood, a badge of his subjugation. A man to have a bit of ribbon pinned to his breast by another man, in token of superiority over his fellows! The degradation is the deeper for its unconsciousness. The tone of manliness is so chronically lowered on the Continent of Europe by the habit of submission to arbitrary state-power, that men of honorable nature are insensible to the dishonor that intrinsically attaches to the wearing of these "decorations," of which they therefore make a peacock-like parade.

The joyous music of young women's laughter, accompanying the martial tramp of numerous strong hoofs in quick gallop, sounds close through the leaves, and I have barely time to yield the better half of the road, when two English girls, superbly mounted, spring by at an Amazonian speed. Their fun seems to be to distance their cavaliers, who strain after them in loud glee. "I say, Harry," cries one of these, evidently enjoying the sport almost as much as a fox-chase, "this is devilish hard work." Four women out of five that one meets on horseback are in swift gallop. Our masculine imaginations make the steed look proud of his beautiful burthen; but for all that, I pity a woman's horse.

Adopting the feminine pace, from the centre of the wood I reach the *Boulevards* in thirty minutes.

—— It is past five when, on my way homeward from the stable, I cross the *Place Vendôme*, where is another of Napoleon's military monuments, the column made of brass cannon taken from the Austrians and Russians in 1805, surmounted by a colossal statue of the Imperial Artilleryman. This column, like most of its author's works, is an imitation of a bad model. In keeping with its borrowed form, the inscription on the base, telling why it was erected, is in Latin. This latinity serves a purpose; for the heartiest admirers of the monument being the ignorant, the unknown tongue, while it sharpens their sense of their own ignorance, will quicken their admiration; and thus, Napoleon is elevated in proportion to their abasement,—which is just as it should be.

Even the cultivated are somewhat imposed upon by Greek or Latin words. These have a big oracular look. The imagination is aroused by the sight of them ere they have spoken. A voice sounding across twenty centuries must be freighted with import. Thus we are apt to infuse into a quotation from those languages a deeper meaning than it ever had; partly too because, no one ever thoroughly understanding a language that he has not learnt through the ear as well as the eye, the imagination, with its practised self-confidence, fills up the void.

—— Nothing exhibits more flagrantly the injustice inherent in civilization than the inequality among the dinners served up to her children; and Paris, by the superlative degree to which she stretches this inequality, deserves the title she assumes of being the capital of the civilized world. Out of her million of inhabitants, more than half can hardly be said to dine at all. In their dark, unfurnished, crowded, infectious lodgings, or, far away from these wretched homes, resting at noon from work, the mechanic and day-laborer appease the gross cravings of hunger with a stinted portion of the plainest, and often unwholesome, innutritious, refuse food. The solace, physical and moral, of a leisurely, abundant repast,—due to every man by Nature, and which Nature is willing and anxious to pay,—this they never have. When two out of three of all who are buried in Paris are so at public cost, and one third die in the hospitals, no especial skill in statistical arithmetic is needed to estimate, without other data, how many of the living daily uphold life by what may be called a dinner; that is a wholesome, sufficing meal. When I put down the dinnerless at six hundred thousand, I am within bounds; and scores of thousands among these would on many days utter in vain the prayer, "Give us this day our daily bread."

Of the remaining four hundred thousand, two consist of small shop-keepers, best-paid mechanics, clerks at low salaries, the inferior class of artists, and others, who although they sit down with a table-cloth, and even napkins, and wine (at 8 cents a bottle), live in the daily habit,—without the virtue,—of obedience to the hygienic prescription of rising from dinner with an appetite.

To make up the million there are two hundred thousand left, comprising capitalists who live on their incomes, computed to be about seven per cent. of the whole population of Paris, the wealthier professional and literary men and artists, the upper *Bourgeoisie*, bankers, traders and large shop-keepers, and the higher office-holders. These are the true diners, the elect (epicureanly speaking), for whom capons were discovered and *riz de veau à la financière*, for whom turbot and oysters of Ostend are brought in ice from the sea, and truffles from the south, and asparagus and strawberries are forced, and *Chambertin* and *Lafitte* exhale their *bouquet*,—men for whom cooks are educated and sauces invented, whose forks come from Potosi and their napkins from Silesia, men who, in our present up-side-down world, stand on that immeasurable height up to which their brother-men gaze with an intensely human longing, and an intensely unchristian sensation,—that predominating eminence, where they are so far above their fellows and the low cares of bread-nourished life, that, without fear of to-morrow, they can to-day spend five to ten francs, and some even twenty or fifty, for a dinner.

To these may be added forty or fifty thousand strangers, permanent and transient; and these are a main stay of the *Restaurants.*

Turning to the left as I issue out of the *rue du Helder* towards six, and walking up the *Boulevard des Italiens* a few hundred yards, I am surrounded by some of the best *Restaurants* of Paris, the *Café de Paris*, the *Maison Dorée*, the *Café Riche*, and on the other side, the *Café Anglais*. At any one of these, at any hour, may be had an impromptu dinner of succulent substantials or of wholesome delicacies, the first course of which will be served, to a man in a hungry hurry, by the time that he has chosen his wine. To-day I disregard their solicitations, and entering the *rue Richelieu* pass under the gateway of No. 112, ascend a short broad stone stairway, and opening a door with the inscription *Cercle de la Conversation*, find myself in the apartment that twenty years ago was widely known as the Frascati gambling-rooms, now occupied by a club, many of whose members are men of letters and artists. Here every day at six a table is laid for twelve or fourteen at three francs and a half, a good French *bourgeois* dinner. Here at a private concert, opened by a witty poem from the spirituel *Mery*, I have heard *Godefroi* on the harp, *Lacombe* on the piano, and *Hermann* on the violin.

This Club deserves its name, being the only one in Paris where there is enough of geniality and of intellectual sociability to create the need of cultivated conversation. In tongue-skirmishing, as in that on the field, the French are rapid and brilliant. Their minds lie near the surface; they dart in and out with a sparkling agility that quickens the wits of all listeners. Just after Lamartine had assumed the control of the journal, *Le Pays*, I asked at dinner a Legitimist opposite (the Legitimists all hate Lamartine)* " Est ce que Monsieur Lamartine a acheté *Le Pays ?*" Without the

* "Has M. Lamartine bought the *Pays ?*"—"No, the *Pays* has bought M. Lamartine."—"Capefigue has a great depth of learning."—"You mean thickness."

pause of a semi-colon he answered, "Non, c'est *Le Pays* qui a acheté M. Lamartine." Some one saying of *Capefigue*, a second-rate historical and political writer, that he had "une grande profondeur de connaissance."—"Vous voulez dire épaisseur," rejoined the same gentleman. I have here heard a French poet conclude a graphic picture of the opening of the battle of Trafalgar by declaring that the signal there thrown out by Nelson,—"England expects every man to do his duty,"—was one of the most sublime incidents in History. I have heard the military infallibility of Napoleon questioned and his tactics criticized, and the pre-eminence of Shakspeare acknowledged. The French have expanded out of their old self-sufficiency; within fifty years they have learnt much from their neighbors and from adversity; from the latter they are just now learning very fast.

Frenchmen are charged with vanity; themselves hardly deny the charge. But this is one cause of their cheerfulness, and of their conversational vivacity; for vanity is a great weaver of cords of connection, which, if not the strongest, are for that the more numerous, and being short and taught, wonderfully enliven superficial personal relations. A man who wishes to attract your regards upon himself, will try to please. That vanity does not necessarily make a man agreeable, and is often a large ingredient in a thoroughly selfish character, we need not go to France to learn. The impulse whereof it is the overgrown fruit, has no root in the heart, it is purely self-seeking; nevertheless, in the composite movement of associated humanity, it plays a functional part. To judge of the heart of a Frenchman, or other man, Paris is not a fair place, for nowhere are men more dwarfed by the pressure of the heartless motto of civilized life—"Every man for himself, and God for us all." This is another testimony in favor of the claim of Paris to be the capital of civilization.

It is not far from eight, when, dinner being some time over, I break off from a pleasant after-chat, and take leave of the Club.

—— * I was introduced to this Club by my friend Henry S. Sanford, Secretary of the United States Legation in Paris. An act of personal kindness I should not thus publish, were not so many of his countrymen under like obligations to Mr. Sanford, that an acknowledgment of them here seems not unbecoming, and will, I am sure, be acceptable to hundreds of Americans, who in the past three or four years have profited by his kindly services.

And here let me add a few words in regard to what is expected of American Legations in Europe.

Some citizens of the United States suppose, that their citizenship entitles them in Europe to the acquaintance and attention of the United States envoys. This is a mistake. A diplomatic agent is a public, not a private servant. So long as the American traveller has no complaint against the public authorities for ill-usage (and even then in most cases the Consul is the proper functionary of whom to seek redress), his claim upon the Envoy has no stronger basis than that upon other American residents in foreign capitals. Equally with the private resident, the Envoy retains the right of expanding or contracting his circle of acquaintance, of choosing his companions, according to his taste or his calculations. If, through inclination or policy, he "entertains," from the greater facility of obtaining introduction to a public than to a private person, a large number of his countrymen will be his guests. But his hospitality lies within the bounds of his reserved private domain. Whether he lives "like a hermit," or "like a prince," is of no concern to any but the small circle to whom the closeness or the openness of his house, is a private loss or a private profit. Princely living was wisely not included in the diplomatic duties of American ministers, by those who established

* These remarks on American Legations, commenced as a note, have stretched so much beyond the expected length, that I have thought it best to include them in the text.

their salaries, and Americans have, as such, no claims on them for balls, dinners, or cards.

What they have a right to expect from them is, that not only should they in their official business, which is little and intermittent, maintain the rights and interests of the United States,—and this they do; but that also in their daily bearing, their habits, tone, conversation, that is, in their unofficial conduct, which is much and not intermittent, they should uphold the principles to which the United States owe their birth, being, and matchless welfare, the principles of political justice, of civic equality, of republican freedom,—and this they do not.

European diplomatic agents in America set an example, which American diplomatic agents in Europe should follow. With rarely an exception, the representatives of foreign governments resident in this country, are unanimous in their condemnation of our institutions, and of all our democratic principles and processes. These feelings of distaste and of oppugnancy to democracy are not concealed: they need not be. These gentlemen represent monarchies and despotisms: their governments are conducted on principles directly hostile to those which rule us. In their opinions, conversation, habits, they manifest the hostility. Hereby their official relations are in no manner obstructed or embittered. They are true to their masters: we acknowledge and respect their right to be so. They keep themselves as European and aristocratic as they can; nobody objects or takes offence.

Now on the contrary, the American diplomatic agent in Europe, instead of keeping American and republican, is no sooner installed, but he sets about to Europeanize and aristocratize himself as much as he can. He bedaubs his carriage with armorial bearings (if not inherited, *improvisêd*); claps livery on his servants; begilds his outside often with more than the official lace;*

* A court-dress with modest gold-lace trimmings, is prescribed by our Government. This should be done away with, as being at war with our

finds as many virtues as possible in the royal family where he is accredited; submits to condescensions from his or her Majesty, or Royal Highness, and even feels himself thereby elevated; affects titled society, and with self-gratulation takes the place which his credentials provide for him as a member of the profligate, arrogant, brazen, soulless, godless circle that surrounds every throne in Europe. But for all his obsequiousness, he and his are admitted no further than the outer halls of this Temple of Belial. Aristocracy is always exclusive, scornful, relentless, as close as freemasonry; and to obtain from it the grasp of fellowship, one must have other credentials than those received from the President of a Democracy.

How different, and how much more consistent, is the bearing of a European envoy. He makes no secret of being bored by people and things, public and private, at Washington. So far from seeking virtues in the Executive body, he scans it with satirical malice; he picks as many holes as he can in the character and intellect of our "great men;" he quizzes our fashion; he sneers at our pretension; and when he quits us, he rejoices in his departure as the end of an exile. The offspring of Monarchy and Aristocracy, he detests our politics and hates our people.

The offspring of Democracy, if true in like manner to his birth and breeding, should regard every Christian king as an usurper, every hereditary privilege as a robbery; and in the presence of royalty and nobility, bedizened in court-tinsel, should feel his moral sense offended, just as is the immoral sense of the diplomatic scion of nobility in presence of the sovereign people in America. The citizen of the United States who has not something of this feeling, is a spurious offspring of the Republic. However he may vaunt his republican home, he has not a discerning, logical appreciation of the blessings he is born to, and is

universal usage in civil costume. Our Legations should be ordered to appear at foreign courts in plain ungilded republican dress.

not fit fully to represent this great self-governing country in prince-ridden Europe. Too many of our envoys have been thus disqualified; and from the commanding position we have now reached as the one great Democracy in the world, hostilely arrayed (in sentiment at least) against the despotisms of Europe,—and the object of their fears, their machinations, their hate,—this disqualification is become the more discreditable to us, and the more hurtful to our true interests. The old and the new are face to face in deadly defiance. We are the new, and whoever represents us in old Europe, should fully feel the nature and significance of this antagonism, and act throughout accordingly.

Instead of living the simple, manly life of hearty republicans, encompassed but not defiled, by aristocratic carnalities; seeking intercourse with those who are at once the ornaments and pillars of a country and the best bonds between their own and other lands, the men of science and culture, and large sympathies; breathing encouragement or consolation into the hearts of the bleeding workers for truth and humanity; instead of this honorable, appropriate, elevated part, which courts by its very heartiness the representatives of the only great Republic in the world, too many American legations are false to their high mission, and, by adopting the thoughts and associations of the implacable foes of freedom, lower the American name in Europe. Aping and otherwise flattering haughty aristocrats, who patronize and sneer at them, and but for the gigantic uplifted arm of Democracy behind, would despise them, they eagerly rush, with the shallow and the idle, into the whirl of oligarchic fashion, and there circle round on the outskirts of the dance of frivolity and vanity, until too soon a change of administration sounds the knell of their recall; when, sighing over the loss of so many Lords, Counts, and Barons, with whom they have sipped champagne and nibbled boned turkey, and sighing still deeper to think, that in exchange for these beribboned and betitled Dons, their associates henceforth are to be militia Colonels and county court Judges, they sadly return home to hog and homony, or pork and molasses.

Leaving the Club,* I drive far up the *Boulevard Poissonnière*, and then turning into a street to the right soon alight at a Café. To one familiar with Cafés on the Boulevards, the plainness of furniture is all that is at first noticeable. There is the usual sprinkling of small tables, brilliant gas-light, and on one side of a long room, the raised desk where presides the universal feminine Divinity, who fingers the cash and deals out sugar and orders. But on calling for beer and segars, to pay for entrance, we find cut on the glasses a red triangle, emblematic of the tripple-phrased republican device. It is a cheap democratic Café where mechanics and laborers meet in the evening for dominos and gossip, and where for a few sous they get a glass of wine or beer with tobacco. This is one of the *salons* of the poor. There are to-day not many visitors, and so after putting into the box, modestly presented by the waiter, a small contribution for imprisoned and exiled democrats, my companion and I withdraw.—In the *marais*, a quarter in the direction of the Faubourg St. Antoine, we alight at another. Here in one large hall are ten billiard tables, nearly all occupied. The players are probably small clerks, journeymen-tailors, and others, whose sedentary vocations earning for them from three to five francs a day, they come here to buy an hour's exercise with that portion of their incomes which continental people, rich and poor, appropriate to amusement. Round the best players are groups of pipe-smoking spectators, and dominos are clattering in other parts of the hall. There is nothing boisterous or rude; an air even of refinement pervades the place. The inmates seem to be thankfully enjoying a rest after the day's work.

* The name and composition of this Club have since been changed, it being now called *Cercle des deux Mondes*, and counting among its members a large number of Americans.

—— It is past nine, when having driven back down the Boulevards, I enter the *Théatre des Variétés*, and take possession of a *stalle d'orchestre* with that pleasant cachinnatory expectation wherewith one seats oneself in a Parisian Comic Theatre.

Flanked by Music and Painting the Histrionic Art here assails the spectator with batteries of fun and pleasantry. The *Théatre Français*, where Molière and Corneille, and the Opera, where Mozart and Bellini preside, live in the high region of æsthetics. But the *Variétés* and its kindred are mostly in their aims too superficial to reach the æsthetic sphere. They deal with facts not with feelings; and their facts are from that omnivorous but uninspired receptacle, the absurd. Though not themselves expressing the profound, their representations have depth of significance. Just beneath the surface where the ridiculous plays its antics, lies a ground of seriousness and sadness. The fantastic figures of the Comic are at times but the flickering flames that shoot through the crust from an intense tragic fire that consumes the core. The absurd is the child of the illogical. The nonconformity to reason and divine law in the fundamental relations of men causes the discords and complications out of which the comic spins its motley web. The truth of comedy is often a demonstration of the falsehood of sober life. Many a spectator here joins in the laugh at a sally, whose piquancy is the crack of the whip wherewith his domestic peace is lashed to death.

At these theatres three or four pieces are given. When the Parisian *Bourgeois* pays for a box, he wishes to spend in it the whole evening, and a long one. The second piece was nearly over when I entered. The third, the beginning whereof was not very sprightly, had proceeded half an hour, when a sudden roar in my ears made me start:—I had fallen asleep, and an electric burst of merriment had waked me. I strove hard to keep my ears alert for the next *double entendre*, but my eyes refusing to back them, I retreated, with the reflection, that a theatre is not the place for one who has worked hard all day. The crowd that I left so wide awake and in a mood so susceptible to fun, had risen late and worked by routine, or not at all.

My day was ended, whether I would or not.

CHAPTER XIX.

A WALK IN THE LOUVRE.

To-day, the 26th of July, 1851, I will take one of my last walks in the Louvre.

Cane or umbrella you surrender in the vestibule, in the basement dedicated to ancient sculpture. Marble walls, marble columns, marble floor, marble statues in spacious lofty halls, overtopped by a palace and enfolded by four feet depth of stone. Here is a Temple consecrated to coolness. The dog-days stay outside with the umbrellas. Correspondent to the physical temperature, the moral air is sedative. A man enraged would quickly subside here: before these empedestalled ghosts he would be ashamed of heat. But you are not depressed, you are tranquillized, you are elevated. Sculpture is serious, not sad; ideal, not servile. The silence, whiteness, solidity, induce meditation. The calm of these figures imparts itself to the beholder; their pensiveness is catching. They stand circumfused, and you with them, by the atmosphere of the world's early days. Vivid and youthful they come from the dim, dead past. They have the weight and dignity of age without its weakness. They are fresh from the heart of Antiquity.

I always go first right through to the Gladiator. For two thousand years those marble limbs have glowed with the splendor of the perfect manly form. In presence of the living human body in this marvellous completeness, your delight in its power, and beauty almost passes into awe; and then, the intensity of sensation is relieved by thoughts on the power and beauty of the human mind that could thus reproduce its own body.

Art is a projection of man out of himself, under the momentum of an effort to appease his yearning for beauty. This creative warmth, when it results, as in this great sculpture, in the reproduction of nature in her selectest proportions and expressions, implies mental elevation and intensity. High Art is the offspring of the craving for perfection—a most noble parentage.

Close by is the Venus of Milo, mutilated of the arms, in whose erect body, sinking as it were into itself, there is as much sleeping strength as voluptuousness. In the head and face, and especially in the mouth, is a world of power. And herein this Venus is higher and truer than the famed one of Cleomenes in the Tribune at Florence. It is a degradation of divine love to present its ideal in a rich body with a poor mental organization. This is to shorten its wings, to materialize its flame, to sensualize it too much. Where the head is so small, as in the statue of the Tribune, all the passions are limited, straitened, belittled. There is no channel for the voluminous flood of love, for its exuberant ardors, no scope for a wide play of its kindling influence, for its deep impregnation of the whole large being with its fire. That it be unfolded in its full richness, it should inflame a glowing strong nature, such as is indicated by this head of the Louvre. In that wealthy mouth there is capacity for more than one passion, and the one that predominates is by this opulence ennobled.

What is the source of the unique perfection in the Grecian type of head? It is, that the brain—itself well proportioned—has generated the face. All the features are finely married to one another and to the forehead. The Grecian face is subordinated to the forehead. Thus the nose is a continuation of the line of the brow, from which it has the air of being directly descended. A Grecian nose pre-supposes a good brow.

The mouth and chin are predominated by the nose ; they neither coarsely project nor weakly retreat. The same with the cheek bones, which are kept back by the intellectual, sensuous superiorities of the forehead, nose and eyes. To say that, in a word, all the parts of head and face are in harmony, were not enough ; for the essence of the Greek ideal is a harmony growing out of the dominance of the superior parts. The Grecian face is not of necessity eminently intellectual, but it cannot be animal. There may be harmony out of the Grecian type, as there may be and is great beauty without prevalence of the Grecian characteristics.

In the Grecian ideal the brow, the lower range of the forehead, is always full, the Greek mind being highly sensuous. In heads and faces the furthest removed from the Greek type, there is no subordination of face to forehead, and no smooth union among the features, nor between them and the brow. Cheek-bones are prominent, or nose and chin independent, or nose is scornful of its neighbors, acknowledging no pre-eminence in the forehead above it, making between itself and the brow a chasm over which it petulantly leaps without the aid of a bridge, or springing out conceitedly from the rest of the face and going on its own hook.

The renowned Diana, sister of the Apollo Belvidere, is here ; but the warm mood which one brings from the Venus is not that most favorable to appreciating the cold beauty of the man-shunning goddess. So, amid marbles less divinely touched, we will pass on to the stairway that leads to the galleries above.

Architecture holds out her magnificent jewelled hand to conduct us from the halls of sculpture to those of painting. The ascent of this grand stairway is an enjoyment like that of gazing at a sculptured or painted masterpiece.

Crossing the graceful, enmarbled Rotunda, at the head of the stairway, we traverse a gorgeous hall more than one hundred feet long, where decorative art has lavished its wealth of gildings and mouldings, and from whose upper end we issue directly into the great octagon room, on the lofty walls whereof are piled up many of the masterpieces of the collection, choice works of the columnar men of Art. Here we cannot now tarry; this is to be the luxurious dessert of our day's feast; so, walking resolutely through this treasure-house, we enter the long gallery, which, being arranged chronologically, opens with the painters of the 14th and 15th centuries, whose greatest merit it is that they were the predecessors and teachers of Leonardo and Raphael. Had they not had such followers, their works would have been unknown. The light from the creations of their great pupils draws them out of darkness. Due honor to them as having made the dawn of an unequalled meridian splendor; but we have not now come to study the development of the art, but to enjoy the products of its ripeness.

In our walk we shall stop before those that in frequent visits have oftenest arrested us; not learnedly to comment on them, but to yield ourselves to the sentiment they awaken, attempting at most to account for the impression made on us, without aiming at critical precision or technical accuracy. Some of unquestionable excellence we shall pass by, and where we do pause, we shall not always have the most words for those we most prize. We go down on the right side.

In the Fine Arts a sentiment, or incident, or person, or passion, must be conveyed into the mind by beauty. If it has not beauty for its vehicle it does not reach the inmost soul, but rests for a time near the surface, whence it is soon effaced. Only in the beautiful is the divine idea vividly present, and therefore only by the beautiful is the human soul deeply wrought and fertilized. To feel this, first stop before this youthful head by the great Leonardo da Vinci, with auburn tresses thickly matted. Without deadening, three centuries have shadowed that beaming brow. Your admiring gaze is met by clear, full, soul-softened eyes. Through a rich smile the closed ample mouth speaks joy, which the eyes second. The up-pointing finger leads your eye to a thin, dim cross held in the other hand, and tells you that you are looking at St. John, whom, but for this emblem you would have taken for a paragon woman, so womanly are the head and face in their contour, benignant expression, and superlative beauty. Drink deeply of this countenance, and carry away as much of it as you can; the whole Empire of Art offers scarcely anything more inspired.

Here is Francis I., by Titian. The large sensuous, sensual head of the luxurious King is in profile, and you at once perceive that this was the best view of him, as it always is of a man of his organization and temperament. This head is charged with electricity; it scintillates with life.

By the side of another superb portrait of Titian is the head of Tintoret, by himself, earnest, grizzly, vigorous.

Artists being the servants of Beauty, which is the twin-sister of Hope, should be hopeful when saddest: they should be optimists. Tragic subjects treated in this transfiguring spirit are rare. Hence I avoid Crucifixions; but it is impossible to pass this small one by Paul Veronese, it stands out in such ghastly clearness against that sickly sky. Only strong genius is equal to this awful theme, so that by the grandeur of the treatment Art bemasters the tragic with the sublime. Even the great Rubens hardly does this; his Crucifixion in the Museum at Antwerp is too terrific. His masterpiece is the Descent from the cross, by some deemed the masterpiece of the world. In a Descent, the agony being over, the heart is not lacerated, and yet the whole feeling of the divine tragedy is brought home.

Venus and Mars, with attendant Cupids, by Lucca Giordano. This little picture is buoyed up by the warmth of its coloring; it seems almost to float on the air. Mark the little Cupids, one of them with a dog, how intent they are on their own play, as if their work was done, and they were taking a holiday.

Cast a glance at the Canalettos and Guardis, with whom canal and quay, marble and water, fluid and solid, are but accessories to exhibit the transparence of a Venitian atmosphere.

We have arrived at the Holy Family, by Murillo, before which we would fain distend our faculty of admiration. The mother is seated, the child Jesus standing on her knee, taking hold of the cross held by the child St. John below, the lamb is on the ground before St. John's feet, the dove over the head of Jesus, and the Father is bending over all from the clouds in an attitude of love and benediction. A rosy freshness with harmony of color, perfect grouping, and an expression from the whole of religious serenity and holy sweetness, hold you before this picture in a state which proves to you the exalting power of Art. The absence of a shining ideal in the heads is made up for by depth of feeling, simplicity, naturalness, and grace.

Hanging next it is a landscape by Collantes, full of Southern richness and Spanish passion.

Here is a Salvator Rosa that would whet an assassin's lust for blood. I don't mean the grand battle-piece, but the stormy landscape, the rock-fronted desolation, with corseletted bandits perched on a precipice.

Walk on until you are stopped by the light which breaks as through a window, from a Holy Family resting in their flight by Albani. Not the first one, but the second, No. 6. [In the first one, No. 5, the landscape is the best.] Winged Angels are offering flowers to the Child, who leans forward from his mother's lap to take them. The landscape looks illuminated by the holy travellers. The figures are wrought with miniature fineness, without weakness. Two Cherubs flying down with a basket of flowers, is a picture within a picture.

We are now in the Rubens' Gallery. This series of colossal canvas exhibits the boundless conception and invention of Rubens. But his hands could not gather up all the wealth that his brain shook down.

Teniers exemplifies the force of truth. Vividly reproduce Nature in full moments, and without your seeking it the electric light of beauty will radiate from your canvas. The Temptation of the Anchorite is such a picture as Burns would have painted, had he worked with pencil. It is sparkling with strength and fun. And so brilliantly executed, such a transparency of light and shade, such reality and vivacity of comic effects. The bearded head of the Anchorite is grand.

Gerard Dow, Ostade, Mieris, express the delight there is in the artistic reproduction of simple, homely objects. With them, Art concentrates itself into microscopic fidelity. But there is something more than this. Look at the Seller of game, by Mieris; it is ideal as well as real, so select is each object, and wrought with such fineness of texture, which fineness is itself a phasis of the beautiful.

At the end of this compartment are the Vandykes. The best one is on the other side. If you wish to be spoken to by a picture, put yourself face to face with the portrait next to the column, the gentleman with open collar and dark velvet doublet.

Before coming upon Wouvermans, there is a single Moucheron, a strip of French elegant rurality, with vases and an orange sky, a glorious segment cut out by genius from Nature's wide landscape.

Two Boths, with skies that are active with life. Whoso can paint the air in motion with sun in it is a master of landscape. That is the key; the rest may by many be acquired; that is the gift. In a picture, as in nature, good air is the first necessary; it vitalizes each tiniest part.

A few steps further is a small Heus, a gem of tone, color, delicacy and truth; warm and happy.

Here is a Cuyp, with shepherds and cows, which warms the whole of the broad canvas it covers. It has the virtue of cheerfulness.

Then we have a wealth of Ruysdaels, Van Bergens, and one Hobbema,* who is the painter of coolness. The Van Bergen next to it glows in contrast with pleasant summer heat.

We pass a number of good Dujardins to get to the better Berghems. There are eight or nine of them, all with sleek cattle and shepherdesses, and all full of health and content. Cattle tell of home and sufficiency. We like to see them thus honored by Art; it pays part of our debt to them.

Amid them is a large Wynants, strong enough to stand its ground in such proximity. Let us not overlook a Vintrank over the last Berghem. It is a sample of modest merit.

We have reached the French department, beginning with a long line of landscapes by Poussin. His pictures want freedom and lightness, and especially they want atmosphere, whereby their grace of composition is blurred. He has been called the learned Poussin. He could never be called the inspired. His pictures are faded; and even the cheerful subjects have a sad look.

The glory of French art is Claude Lorrain, the lustrous, as he might be termed. He has visited the sun, and brought away the secret of its light. His pictures are heated by so natural a fervor, that it seems supernatural. It looks not like art, but intuition. But besides this there is an unfading grace in his forms, whether of hill, tree, bridge or building. His water is luminous.

Go to the end of the gallery for the sake of a head by Lefevre. In this head is the mystery of all great portraits. The features and flesh are transparent by means of a light burning within, which makes the blood tingle to the surface.

We have walked fourteen hundred feet in a straight line; we will return on the other side.

Pass the long, stiff, uniform regiment of lifeless Lesueurs, and

* My friend, Thomas J. Bryan, of Philadelphia, for many years a resident of Paris, has in his collection a Hobbema of higher quality than this one.

only stop for a moment before a head by Ferdinand Bol, in which students of Harvard of a quarter of a century back will recognize good President Kirkland energized.

A few steps further is the exquisite Vanderfelde, an evening cattle-piece, with the purple-tinted sky reflected in the glassy water.

We skip a long file to get to a portrait before which I always linger longer than before any other in the Louvre, No. 389, by Phillipe de Champagne. The lips are slightly parted, for there is more life within than could be supported by breathing through one inlet. From the polish on the hair to the dew of the eye, there is everywhere inflation of life. The flesh has the pulpy look that belongs to an in-door man, and the transparent hand knows of no rough handlings. Pause here still to wonder at the vivifying power there is in the fingers of man when moved by a genial brain.

Next we have three landscapes by Pynaker, three graces. Here are skies as warm and lively as Claude Lorrain's; not so dazzling, because freshened by more northern clouds and less expansive. Every object is rounded by the mellow ripening air. Clover is growing sweeter every hour, and peaches more juicy. The distances are as true as an Indian's sight.

Stop before a fruit-piece by Mignon, the one with the melon and the red Indian corn, and the summer ripeness and luxuriance. To judge from a glimpse we get through a leaf-darkened arch, the landscape beyond is fine, but is shut out by overgrowth of August foliage.

Six naked children dancing in a ring, hand in hand, to music by a maiden on a triangle, by Giraud de Lairesse. The treatment is not equal to the conception and composition, and to the sensibility denoted by the choice of subject.

Three landscapes by Asselyn, which might serve as pendants to those of Pynaker.

Next to these is a nest of Poelembergs, who should be styled the pearly. A practised discernment might, one would think, in the characteristics of the work, detect those of the artist. Yet the engraved portrait of Poelemberg is not at all wanting in boldness and virility, while his pictures look as though the hand that painted them had been as soft as that of a petted woman.

I am not attracted by architectural pictures, but I cannot pass by Pannini's interior of St. Peter's at Rome, painted on a canvas about seven feet by five. The elevation, the vastness, the richness, the spaciousness, the play of light through gigantic arches, the grandeur and gorgeousness of the marble world, all is there.

It is wearing late, and the large hall awaits us. We must hasten by the Carraccis and the Guidos, the tears in the eyes of whose upturned feminine faces are drops distilled from the serenest depths of Heaven. But here is a countenance we can never pass without a greeting. Look at that youthful, mild, thoughtful, beardless, beautiful, womanly, profound face. Coleridge somewhere says that high poetic genius is largely feminine. The mind of universal sympathies has twofold elements. The type and exponent of humanity, it partakes of woman's as well as man's nature. The truth of this is exemplified in the picture before us, and in the character of him of whom it is the portrait. It is that of the youthful Raphael,

> ——— that beaming face,
> Where intellect is wed to grace.

Now we are back to the octagon Hall, seated before the vast renowned Paul Veronese, the Feast of Cana. This picture represents not a solemn miracle, but a pleasant festival; it is agreeable, not great. Its merits are in coloring and individualities; as a whole it is prosaic. Neither the head nor the position of Jesus is predominant. But for the glory, it would hardly be recognized. The foreground is filled by the musicians, who should be nowhere visible. The two wings of the table pull the eyes from one to the other across the wide canvas. In a sacred subject such gross anachronisms of costume and architecture are not allowable. Take away the Christ, and the picture becomes more satisfactory. It has not the elevation and holiness which that subduing presence should shed, whatever the subject.

Two hours of standing and walking, with eyes and brain stretched before scores of differing mind-moving objects, drain the nervous reservoir. It has just replenished itself by a delicious slumber of twenty minutes, whereto the deep, springy, soft-backed ottoman was accessory. A day-sleep I never enjoyed more than this, and rise up re-animated to finish my grateful task.

The master is shown by the selection of subjects, and then by his mastery in treatment over a good choice. Capability of grace is the highest test of a pictorial subject. The artist having the insight and sensibility to appreciate this test, his next step is to make the most of this capability in his execution. Look at the Correggio on the left of the Supper of Cana. Here is grace in forms, in attitude, in grouping, in expression.

Beauty does not necessarily involve grace. Grace is the matrix of beauty, but the offspring sometimes neglects the parent. Grace is the finer essence, an emanation or a movement which is more than corporeal beauty. "The beautiful," says Plato, "is the splendor of the true." The graceful may be called the spirit of the beautiful. Grace is always beautiful, but beauty is not always graceful.

Contrast with this divine Correggio the Giorgione next to it. Those two nude female figures look as though they had been fatted for roasting.

Talent cannot reveal, it can only perceive what is already revealed; new things it invests with old forms. Genius not only reveals, but to old things it gives a new face. See that Raphael, the winged St. Michael descending, spear-pointed, upon the prostrated Devil. Here is grandeur magnified, simplicity ennobled, by grace. What lightness in the down-flashing angel, and at the same time what power; how strength is spiritualized by beauty. The wings here give impetus to the blow. Wings help a descending figure; but when the figure ascends, their inadequacy to lift the human body will mingle in and weaken the effect. The wings idealize the combat, which without them would be prosaic, like all combats, the which are therefore subordinate subjects of Art. The cultivated sensibility, which in health rejects real horrors, digests easily the factitious when handled in this style. In Raphael as in Shakspeare instinct and judgment work together.

The Correggio opposite, Antiope and Jupiter in form of a satyr, with its glittering beauty in the head and limbs of Antiope, falls short of perfection from the ungraceful foreshortened position of the body.

The comic dispenses with grace, or rather it veils it with a playful mask. In the corner is an Ostade, wherein is more of the comic than probably the artist intended. It is a schoolroom, with urchins at anything but their books, and presents a quiet rich contrast between pedagogy and nature, between compulsion and liberty, the teacher being the most compelled. What transparence, individuality, reality. The light goes into every corner, and the shadows too are everywhere. You can measure the dimensions of the room.

Further to the left is a Solario, a Mother suckling her child, before the which you can commit no extravagance of praise, such a clustering of beauties is there. You think the mother's face the most beautiful you ever saw, so beaming is it with maternal joy. Then fix your look on the infant, holding, in the playful fulness of life, one foot in his hand. After you have wondered at the creative efficacy of Art, cap your admiration with a gaze into his half-closed eye. I know not what is the judgment of traditional criticism on this picture, but to me it is one of the master-works of the Louvre.

We pass a female head of Rembrandt, glowing in the golden mist that he steeps his heads in, and pause before a Raphael beside it, another maternal incarnation, and we let the breath of genius inflate enthusiasm till it floods. Here is a rainbow of expression whose feet are the countenances of the ecstatic St. John and the sleeping child, and its arch that of the benignant mother.

Next is another woman. But here is no deep emotion inspiring the countenance. There is no sparkling flush of feeling on the surface. The soul is not out on the face, it sleeps behind. Gaze, and you will become aware of it, and at the same time not wish it more revealed. The power of beauty here suffices; its excess is its inspiration. Anything more were too much, and would overcome the artist. This is beauty in its calm splendor, in its dazzling ripeness. It is "Titian's Mistress."

Beauty in Art, itself the highest artistic creation, is in turn creative, inbreeding in the beholder new thoughts, dilating him into a higher, happier susceptibility.

CHAPTER XX.

FRAGMENTS.

In one of the "Latter Day Pamphlets," Mr. Carlyle asks tauntingly, what have the Americans done?—We have abolished Monarchy, we have abolished Aristocracy; we have sundered Church and State; we have so wrought with our English inheritance, that most Englishmen better their condition by quitting the old home and coming to the new. We have consolidated a State, under whose disinterested guardianship the cabined and straitened of the old world find enlargement and prosperity. We have suppressed standing armies; we have decentralized government to an extent that before our experiment was deemed hopeless; we have grown with such a dream-like rapidity, as to stand, after little more than a half-century of national existence, prominent on the earth among the nations; and this, through the wisdom of political organization, whereby such scope is given to industry and invention, that not only are our native means profitably developed, but the great influx of Europeans is healthfully absorbed. We have in fifty years put between the Atlantic and the Pacific an Empire of twenty-five millions, who work more than any twenty-five millions on earth, and read more than any other fifty millions. We have built a State at once so solid and flexible, that it protects all without oppressing any. Our land is a hope and a refuge to the king-crushed laborers of Europe, and from the eminence above all other lands to which it has ascended, by our forecast, vigor, and freedom, it is to the thinker a demonstration of the upward movement of Christendom, and a justification of hopes that look to still higher elevations.

Mr. Carlyle's sneers at our lack of heroism would be unworthy of him, from their very silliness, were they not more so from their sour injustice. Let any People recite its heroic deeds, on flood or field, since we were a nation, and we will match every one of them. And in the private sphere, where self-sacrifice, devotion, courage, find such scope for heroic virtues, our social life is warm with them. But this is no theme for words. For his unworthy ones, we deem well enough of Mr. Carlyle to believe, that, when disengaged from the morbidly subjective, and therefore blinding and demoralizing moods, to which he is liable, he is ashamed of having printed them. It looks somewhat as though this passage had been written just to give us an opportunity of victorious retort, or to tempt us into an exhibition of our national propensity to brag,—a propensity, be it said, which is national in every nation we know anything of, whether English, French, German, or Italian. We only beat them in bragging, just as we beat them in ploughs and statues, in clippers and steamboats, in whalemen and electric telegraphs, in cheap newspapers and cheap government. They all do their best at bragging, and so do we,—and we beat them.

The mummies of Egypt are a type of conservatism,—a childish effort to perpetuate corporeal bulk, to eternize the perishable, to subordinate essence to form, to deny death. The result is a mummy.

It were hard to say, whether in this "villainous world" there is more of malignant censure, or of unclean praise.

Hereditary aristocrats are puppets to whom motion is imparted by wires, inserted under ground into the dead bones of their forefathers.

In England, money is the only means wherewith to get what is called a "good education." The best is poor enough, to be sure. For want of culture, the minds and souls of the masses stagnate in a brutish obscurity, or blindly stir in a chaotic twilight. Thus are the noblest and highest faculties in man dependent for their unfolding and growth, on gold,—gold, which in our present society, is ever obtained by accident, by self-immolation, or by fraud. The treasure of God is in the keeping of Mammon.—With us, public schools greatly assuage this evil.

In civilized life,—which is a universal battle,—truth forms the reserve, and is only brought up at critical junctures.

There are spiritual egotists, people who self-complacently assume to be the elected of God. The humility of such is a weed nourished in the rank soil of pride; their belief is mostly an induration on the fancy of a shallow nature.

Many of the self-righteous are not only proud of their supposed nearness to God, but assume towards him patronizing airs; so monstrous are the effects of pride in combination with religion.

Music is a marriage of the sensual with the spiritual. Each is merged in the other. In perfect harmony there will be neither sensual nor spiritual, but the two will be made one in the fulness of life and purity.

One has at times the desire to cast away one's personality, with all the petty memories and imaginations that cling around self, and to bound off into the empyrium of the Universal. Thus disencumbered, the Intellect and Soul might make great discoveries. Is not this the secret of the far-seeing glances of some of the mesmerized, that they are emancipated from the bonds of self, and for the time lifted out of the obscurities of fleshly life, into the translucent sphere of the disembodied ?

Galileo calls doubt the father of inventions.

The practical might imparted by integrity is seldom fully valued. Hence Washington is underrated by some men, who judge him by his intellect and prudence.

Our habitation, the Earth, is not self-subsisting ; it moves in dependence on a heavenly body far distant. The Sun's light helps to feed the breath of our bodies ; and shall we from the soil beneath our feet, from the dust into which our bodies dissolve, draw the breath of our souls ? If millions of miles off is one of the chief sustainers of our flesh, where should we look for the source of the spirit we feel within us ?

When a man's conversation consists chiefly of reminiscence, he may be said to talk backwards.

People in high places who are not beneficent, are out of place on an elevation.

When there have been great examples of virtue, revealing the capabilities of human nature, crime in the powerful is more criminal than in earlier inexperienced times. The selfishness of Napoleon is more repugnant than that of Cæsar.

In many cases when people speak of their conscience, conceit is mistaken for conscience

When man is young, the whence he is and the mysteriousness of his being possess his nascent thoughts. Later, he occupies himself about the object and ends of his existence. Hence the religious dreams of nations in their youth ; and the philosophies of nations that are cultivated.

Preaching is in these days not unlike shovelling sand with a pitchfork.

Men whose masterly vigor was the servant of expediency not of principle, self-seekers not truth-seekers, liars in act and in thought, were Cromwell and Bonaparte.

The Hebrews mounted to the idea of unity ; but their God was revengeful, " a jealous God," and therefore false and sub-human.

The Greeks were more intellectual and much more æsthetic than the Hebrews ; yet one cannot conceive of Christianity originating in polytheistic Greece, it could only spring up in monotheistic Judea.

To the opinions and creeds they have received from their fathers men hold as to the houses and lands they have inherited. Conservatism is a sort of materialism, men confounding the spiritual with the material, and treating him who takes away their opinions like him who steals their cattle ; in their density not perceiving that, instead of a theft, the destruction of their opinions is a barter whereby they may gain a hundred-fold. Thoughts are subject to higher laws than things.

Beliefs imply non-beliefs. Creeds are compounded mainly of negations.

The remedy for England is to turn, not her waste lands to use, but her waste mind, her waste intellect and feeling. This, the most precious domain she possesses, is half tilled in patches.

Good rhetoric is a good thing in a good cause.

By continuous breach of the moral law, men forfeit mental growth. Napoleon and Cromwell grew not wiser as they grew older. Their minds did not ripen, they petrified.

On the Continent of Europe it looks as though government had been made first, and man afterwards.

The great recent discoveries of Gall, of Fourier, of Priesnitz, all combine to make apparent the resources, the incalculable vigors, the inborn sufficiency of man.

In England so many people look as though they were waiting for my lord.

That with all the mind's achievements, practical and poetical, its conquests in science, its Christian and intellectual development, its many enlargements and emancipations, there still should be so much evil, so much misery, proves how wide a swing mankind must make to fulfil its destiny. Hereby are denoted opulence, and depth, and complexity of power.

In this light, evil is a whip to urge moral effort up to high tension. Society perfects itself through tribulation. Man may be figured as at first lying in the low places of life, with but dim sparse glimmerings into upper fields. Out of a night of animal being, little by little he struggles into the day of a wider humanity, his struggles getting fiercer as he rises. As feeling and thought unfold themselves, his inward conflicts grow warmer and deeper. The grandeurs of his nature loom out as much in endurance as in action. The terrible, the pathetic, the sublime, are the great offspring of his throes, the tokens of his splendor and his resources. Through this stormy region, darkened by chasms and abysses, he ascends to one more serene, where, under influences wrought out by his higher self, he breathes an atmosphere predominated by spiritual elements. He grows in intellect by working with Nature in her richest fields; and with his heart purified by beauty, and enlarged and strengthened into freer communion with God, he attains at last to a blessed activity, a creative calm.

Shakspeare's words, when boldest and richest, are but ambassadors, behind whom there is a greater than themselves. Racine's and Afieri's, though not so erect and gorgeous, are the Kings themselves, and thus leave nothing untold, and feed not the imagination.

To see things as they are, one must have sympathy with the Spirit of God, whence all things come. Then can be discerned to what degree there is remoteness from original design, and thus actual conditions be rightly judged.

In the style of Shakspeare there is an oceanic undulation. In that of Corneille and Racine the surface is level, or if broken, it is with furrows, not with billows.

In poetry, much of the meaning is conveyed by the sound. Transpose the words of a fine passage, and you impair its import.

You may gather a rainbow out of one of Rubens's great pictures.

A sonnet should be like a spring, in being clear and deep in proportion to its surface; and like a whirlpool, in a certain silent self-involved movement.

The mind is defiled that comments habitually on the vices of others. One that is undefiled, cannot long endure the fumes that arise from the stirring of moral filth.

When a man readily gives ear to a calumny, he betrays fellow-feeling with the malignity whence it sprang.

Forms soon waste the substance they are designed to hold. Thus ceremony and hypocritical corporeal salutations get to be a substitute for genuine politeness; religion is crushed under a burthen of ritual observances; paper-money drives out metal, to represent which, it was invented.

Some of Wordsworth's poetry is, like his person, too gaunt; it wants a fuller clothing of flesh.

Many of the old monasteries were founded by repentant reprobates; and the early sins of their founders seem to have borne fuller crops, than their latter virtues.

Every now and then a woman sallies boldly into our territory; as if she wanted to make reprisals on the tailors.

When you build selfishly, you build frailly. When your acts are hostile to the broad interests of your fellow-men, they are seed which will one day come up weeds, to choke your own harvest-field.

A man with wounded feelings walks into the country, and there the perfumes and sweet aspects of Nature accost his heart with consolation.

Rhymes should sit as lightly on verse, as flowers on plants.

Poetry is not put into verse to please the ear; it is in verse because it is the offspring of a spirit akin to that which dwells ever in hearing of the music of the spheres. To poetry, rhythm is as natural, as symmetry to a beautiful face. Genuine verse pleases the ear, because like the voice of childhood or of woman, it is in itself delightful. The setting sun, a lively landscape, a noble deed, give pleasure, because they speak to and are in harmony with our higher being; and so is poetry, and therefore it too gives pleasure. But to say, that the object of poetry is to give pleasure, is to rank it with the shallow inventions of the showman.

In the drama, the incidents should all grow out of the characters. Individual characterization is the mystery of the drama. He who does not unlock this mystery, fails to achieve a genuine drama, whatever may be his other excellencies.

The strong genius who rules, as strong genius always does, his fellows, feeds them from the common springs of humanity, with evil or with good, through the vast channels of his own mind. If himself evil, the evil of his time sways his contemporaries through him. Into himself he collects the black vapors of falsehood, and blasts them forth over the world or his country, with a tempestuous power, before which the good and the true shrink for a time into privacy and silence. But what he does, however stupendous, lacks life; for evil cannot create, it can only obstruct or arrest creative good.

The poet is the pupil of truth; for the false can never be poetry.

The dramatic writer, says Lessing, as his production is to be seen as well as heard, is somewhat under the restrictions of the painter.

Lessing, who may almost be called the father of modern criticism, thinks that the chief cause of the inferiority of the Romans in tragedy, was their gladiatorial combats. In the words of De Quincey, who has adopted this opinion, "the amphitheatre extinguished the theatre."

In sunny, fruitful, populous Italy, naught is so alive as the voice of the long-dead Dante. Sick at heart, the Italian, prince-ridden and priest-ridden, goes to his home, saddened by the execution, or imprisonment, or exile of a son or brother, and there, to fly from the present, he opens his Dante;—and soon his pulse beats strong again, and his eye glistens, and he gains assurance of his own manhood, and he hopes and he dares.

Where in English Prose is there a diction so copious, apt, forceful, as Carlyle's, at once so transparent with poetic light and so compact with a home-driving, idiomatic solidity, doing the errand of a thoughtful fervent nature with such fulness and emphasis?

Possibly the mind cannot, in its most far-piercing imaginations, outrun its capabilities. Were it a law of being, that the brightest flowers, unfolded in the sun of the heart's warmest day-dreams, contain the seeds of substantial realities?

Just ideas are the only source of healthy moral life; by them are institutions moulded, and to uphold institutions which ideas have outgrown, is to be destructive, not conservative. They are the highest benefactors of their race who can discern and apply the deepest ideas; and thus the boldest reformer may be the truest conservative.

The Greeks and the English seem to be the only two nations possessing enough sap and vigor and fulness of nature, to reproduce themselves in distant soils, through colonists that swarmed off from the parent hive.

What power there is in belief, and what power in falsehood, in our sensual organization of society, that sinful, semi-pagan Rome is still the so-called spiritual head of the half of Christendom.

In Italy the living is clewed to the dead: the carcass of the past lies athwart the legs of the present.

The increasing delight in Natural Scenery is one of the proofs that man is growing nearer to God.

We talk of this man's style and that man's, when, rightly speaking, neither of them has a style. Style implies a substantial body of self-evolved thought. The mode and quality of the clothing in words and phrases to this original body constitutes style. Now, from so few minds come fresh emanations, that most writings are but old matter re-worded, current thought re-dressed. Each one's individual mode of re-wording and re-dressing is, and should be called, his *manner*, not his *style*. In Writing as in Painting, every man, the weakest as well as the strongest, must have a manner, but few can have a style.

To be sought and cherished is the man whose mind is too large to be filled by creeds and systems, and too generous to close itself against any wants of humanity. The mental home of the true man is among principles, and principles are infinitely expansive.

People nominally worship God one day in the week, and really worship Mammon seven.

The grand and sublime are in the exuberance of rudimental energy. Heaving and glowing with creative power, they stand apart, too stern to coalesce, too overbearing for harmony. They are Strength not yet married to Grace. Hence they generally precede the beautiful. Phidias came before Praxiteles, Michael Angelo before Raphael, Æschylus before Sophocles.

1st Boy (tauntingly). Who was that man with your father?

2d Boy. That man's worth more than your father.

1st Boy. He was drunk, anyhow.

2d Boy. He's worth two houses.

1st Boy (worsted). Ho, I guess my father's worth two houses, too. (Street dialogue, Newport, R. I., Jan. 26, 1848.)

St. Augustine calls Homer, "Sweet liar."

The Bible should be studied with activity of spirit. Its great heart will not beat but to the throbbing of yours. Just to read it passively, traditionally, dulls the very susceptibility through which it is to be taken in. Not thus will you find God in the Bible. Who has not first sought him in his own heart and in the life around him, will scarcely find him there at all. God is not locked up in the Bible: he is at all times around, within us. Strive with Jesus to feel his presence. Then you may hope for purification, for inspiration: then your heart may produce biblical chapters. For what is in the Bible came out of the human soul, touched to inspired utterances by the awakened inward divinity.

The Priests of Rome discourage intercourse with God through the Bible, which is already at one remove. Themselves they constitute the sole interpreters of the divine, the sole medium of communication between God and man. The divine essence they would first distil through the foul alembic of their brazen egotism. Hence, where they long dominate, religion becomes materialized, and for uplifting, soul-purging knowledge of God, is substituted abasing, sensual submission to priesthood.

Widely and kindly around us must we look as well as inwardly and upwardly, or we leave untenanted some of the heart's best chambers. Our breasts are large enough to entertain multitudes, and only when thus filled is our daily life a full blessing.

Our poor social organization engenders vacuums, which are apt to fill with wind. Hence, most of Northern "abolitionism," and other pseudo-philanthropies. Many people are not comfortable without pets or hobbies. It is not the poor African that is the pet,—would that it were,—but a something abstract, an ideal formula, a pet of the mind. That it cannot become concrete, is its chief qualification as a hobby. It can be ridden the more showily and at the same time safely. Snuffing perfume from the fields sown by a philanthropized imagination, the rider careers along with a plethoric self-complacency, and really believes that he is doing something. And so he is, in truth, but something different from what he believes. This class of people have discovered the secret of making virtue easy.

An ape is a creature who has approached the gates of reason, and stands there grinning and jabbering in tragi-comical ignorance of his nearness to the regal palace.

Religious humility is apt to be accompanied by personal arrogance.

So luminous and creative is the mind, that what is brought to it through the imagination is often more stirring than the same presented by the senses. Hence, some scenes are more exciting if well told, than if actually beheld. The mind magnifies and adorns them in its immeasurable chambers.

We seek happiness by heaping on our puny selves all we can, each one building, according to the joint force of his intellect and selfishness, a reversed pyramid, under the which the higher it rises the lower he is crushed on the small spot his small self can fill.

We are capable of life-long joy. Continuous, varied enjoyment might be the sum of earthly existence. If our lives will not bring out this sum, it is because men have misplaced, or mislaid, or overlooked, or misreckoned with some of the counters.

When we sow the best fields of life with our appetites, we cannot but reap hates and fears. Blighting disappointment comes from thwarted greeds, from frustrated self-seeking.

A fit ideal embodiment of the artist were a countenance upraised, beaming, eager, joyful, moulded with somewhat of feminine mobility.

Goethe goes out of himself into the being of natural objects. Wordsworth takes their being up into himself. These two poets illustrate sharply the difference between the *objective* and the *subjective*.

Envy, like venomous reptiles, can only strike at short distances.

There is no deeper law of nature than that of change.

A book should be a distillation.

Everything that we do being a cause, he is the most sagacious who so does that each cause shall have its good effect. This practical long-sightedness is wisdom, the want of it foolishness. To-days are all fathers of to-morrows, but like many other fathers, they sadly neglect their paternal duties. To-day, if it thinks at all, thinks of itself, and leaves to-morrow to take care of itself. Life is a daily laying of eggs, some to be hatched to-morrow, some next month, some next year, some next century. Many are not hatched at all, but rot or are broken; many come prematurely out of the shell, and perish from debility; and thus that much life is wasted. Charity is long-sighted, selfishness is short-sighted. And yet, so defective is our social constitution, that a man may be long-sighted in using his neighbor for his own ends. Thus doctors,—who are short-sighted when they take their own physic, which they seldom do,—are long-sighted when they give it to their patients; for the more of it these take, the oftener the doctor is called. It were a mistake to suppose that parsons are long-sighted because they set their minds so much upon the next world; their long-sightedness consists in directing other people's thoughts to that quarter, while from the super-mundane spectators they draw the wherewithal to be content with this.—Lawyers are short-sighted when they encourage litigation; the long-sighted know that the perverted passions of civilized men will bring grist enough to their mill without their stir.—Tailors intend to be long-sighted when they stitch on your buttons instead of sewing them.—The man who sells rum is short-sighted, but less so than he who drinks it.—Authors are very short-sighted when they write to please the public, instead of writing to please the truth.—Expedients are short-sighted, principles long-sighted; and notwithstanding the apparent prosperity of some liars, nothing is so long-sighted as truth.

In the plainest of Wordsworth's many hundred sonnets there is more or less of the fragrant essence of high humanity.

To write a good book on any subject requires the "instinct of the beautiful."

"You cannot serve God and Mammon:" nay, you cannot serve yourself and Mammon.

To weave the wondrous form wherewith life invests itself in humanity, the heart works ceaselessly, and every organ, member, part and particle of the living frame works, each joyfully in its sphere, in unison with the heart, for the maintenance of the common fabric. But a continuation and extension of the unconscious labor of the heart and lungs is the conscious work of the head and hand of man, whose end is, to feed, to clothe, to lodge, to develop, to delight his body and his mind. All labor, the unconscious and the conscious, is but life methodized, that is, life made more living, more intelligent, and thence more productive. And thus labor, which is the condition and result of life, becomes the means of its perpetuation, its extension, its elevation. All labor may be delightful; and as, the healthier the body is, the more joyfully and thoroughly the heart and its allies perform their unconscious work, so in a healthy social organization all labor, the greatest and the least, ceasing to be repulsive and becoming attractive and delightful, would be proportionately productive. A consummation this not barely most devoutly to be wished, but most surely to be accomplished, by that high labor which the intellect exalted by love and faith is equal to performing.

The ideas of eternity and infinity are innate in the human mind as attractions towards perfection, as indications and promises of incalculable elevation.

The subjects of old European Monarchies inherit from the past such a load of debt, of slow-paced customs, of lazy monopolies, and other cold drawbacks from behind, that they cannot move forward. Instead of briskly turning the now, the to-day, to rich account, they have to work first against yesterday, to stave it off with its manifold pressure. Hence, half the laborers of England, Germany, France, earn not for themselves food, clothing and lodging enough to keep out hunger and cold. Their hands are mortgaged to the past. Their existence has no new life in it; it is a lingering perpetuation of the past. Whereas we of democratic America let not the past accumulate upon us. For us, sufficient for the day is the evil thereof. We make clean work as we go. We keep the present lively, because we are ever snatching a new present from across the confines of the future. We are always "going ahead;" that is, building up the Future out of itself and not out of the past. We don't wait for the Future, we rush in pursuit of it.

The higher the sphere the greater the freedom. Mineral, vegetable, animal; zoophite, reptile, quadruped, man; savage, barbarian, civilized. Each of these series is an ascension towards freedom, the highest being the freest.

Religion, above all things, needs to be steadied and purified by science and culture.

Classification is the highest function of intellect; it brings order out of chaos. It is both analysis and synthesis. The higher the department of universal life, the keener of course must be the intellectual insight that could detect its organic law. To order minerals is feebler work than to order morals. The man who classes, needs to have a kind of creative mastery over his material. He intellectually recreates it. The savage, who has mastery over nothing, but is a brute serf of Nature, has scarcely any power of classification.

Thought is ever unfolding. A good thinker keeps thinking.

As with the body 'tis a sign of derangement, if the action of any organ makes itself felt, the motions of the heart, for example, or the laboring of the stomach; so too with the mind, the protracted consciousness of any feeling is unhealthy, whether it be the religious sentiment or the lust of revenge.

Who fears the forces of Nature? We use them for our profit: the stronger they are, the more profitable we make them. The passions of man, all his feelings, impulses and motives to action, are similarly innocent and available. They are the strongest forces and instruments in Nature. We must learn only to use them.

We must be realists, not dreamers; we must found our convictions on facts, not on imaginations which are dream-like. Nothing is nobler than facts. Facts are God's; imaginations are man's, and are only then god-like, when they enfold coming or possible facts, or adorn existing ones.

The spokes of the wheel are helpless until bound together by the rim.

Christianity promises such moral splendors, that men, refusing to credit these as an earthly possibility, translate its consummations to the super-mundane sphere. Priestcraft has always fostered this incredulity, which opens to it the imagination as its work-field, where the tillage is much lighter than on a tangible soil. It is easier to saw air than to saw wood; easier to put the wretched off with sanctimonious assurances of celestial compensations, than to wrestle with earthly ills, and by wisely opposing, end them; easier to preach of Heaven to come, than to put hand to work to drive off a present hell. The conscientious pastor knows, how almost fruitless a task it is, when, not content with stale ritual repetitions and wordy exhortations, he labors practically to purge and vivify his flock. With all his toil he brings little to pass. His theological tools are dull; what steel there ever was in them is worn off.

Nature rejects with contempt an hereditary aristocracy.

In our present mis-organized society, helplessness is the condition, not of nine in ten, but of all. The wisest and wealthiest are encompassed by exposure, dangers, calamity. Against earthly troubles, resignation and ultra-terrene expectation are a poor resource, as illogical as meagre. What is done on earth is of our own making or allowing. Heaven is just, and inflicts naught. It lets us do for our good or evil, and when we help ourselves, helps us. Put we our shoulders to the wheel, the Hercules is instantly at our side. We make the beds we lie in; not you or I, but you and I, and all the you's and I's that surround us. Against our needs and woes, you *or* I can do little, but you *and* I, everything. Association, which has made railroads and banks, can do much better and higher.

As its roots spread and strike down, the tree expands and mounts. Thoughts and aims are only then sound, when their roots are firm in the earth. The rest is brain-sick fancy, conceited delusion. The earth and our bodies are for the mind and heart to grow and revel in. When we would sacrifice the God-given earth and its joys to a tinsel manufacture which we miscall Heaven, we stigmatize Providence, and supplant it with our puling fantasies.

But people do not so sacrifice; they only make themselves bootlessly wretched by vainly striving to do so. This short-sighted effort is for the behoof of the priest, who, three times in four, is but a broker who drives a belly-filling business by exchanging drafts on the next world for coin that buys the comforts of this.

There is nothing that some people are more ignorant of, than their own ignorance.

The classification of England's inhabitants into nobility, gentry, shop-keepers, mechanics, laborers, paupers, is as consonant to nature as would be the classing of animals according to weight and color.

Fourier undertakes to make all men honest. No wonder that he is looked upon as a visionary, who promises so stupendous a revolution in human affairs.

An unsightly object is an old face haunted by the vices of youth.

Credulity is a characteristic of weakness. Imagination precedes Reason. Fancies are a loose substitute for knowledge. Hence the unreasonable creeds of young nations, fastened upon them by priestcraft, whose criminal practice it has been, and is still, by terrifying the imagination to subjugate the reason. The first-born of priestcraft was the Devil.

Priests are ever shuffling over the leaves of old books: the life there may be in these they petrify with their own hardness: they seek God in traditions and hearsays, and the dim utterances of the livers of old: they abide by the outgivings of obsolete mystics: they re-assert the beliefs of antiquated seers: the ecstasies of feverish hallucination they endorse as imperative dogmas. They grovel and grope in the darkness and dawn, to find stakes planted by the crude beginners of the world, to the which, by grossest cords, they would bind to the past our forward-reaching souls. The future, too, they suborn and would monopolize: with their contemptible Heavens and ridiculous Hells, they would captivate our hopes and our fears. Out of imaginations that are shallow, unhallowed, meagre, foul, they impudently construct both the past and the future. That they may be paid for furnishing rush-lights, they cultivate darkness, and be-curtain with creeds and dogmas the human tabernacle against the sun of truth. Those who appeal to the God of light, and to the upright soul of man, against their sophistications and usurpations, they crucify. Audaciously they dub themselves the ministers of God, they who are especially not God's ministers but men's. Spiritual insight, moral elevation, rich sympathies, these are the tokens whereby the divinely ordained are signalized. Are candidates for any priesthood admitted or rejected by these signs? Not by inborn superiorities of sensibility, but by acquired proficiencies, by intellectual adoptions are they tested. This creed, these articles, this ritual,—do they accept these, then are they accepted. To be learned in humanity, a living learning, which the large heart imbibes without labor, this is not their title; but to be learned in theology, a lifeless learning, which the small head can acquire by methodical effort. They would live and make others live by the dead letter, and not by the living law. The dead letter is the carcass of what has been, or what is imagined to have been. The living law is what is: it is not written, it is forever being written on the heart of man by the hand of God.

What by defect of harmonious organization Christendom wastes of nervous power would vitalize a planet.

Machinery and the useful Arts are man's inventions for industrial helps. The Fine Arts he creates for æsthetic helps.

Disproportion is disqualification. Too much is unwieldy: too little is feebleness. A giant is of no more use than a dwarf. A man seven feet high finds his extra foot a daily incumbrance. A man of more head than heart is dangerous: a man of more heart than head is a victim.

Every deed of man is preceded by a thought. In the most trivial movement, immaterial action is the antecedent and producer of the material. Every result brought about by human contrivance and will is an embodied finishing whose beginning is a spiritual seed sown in the brain. No grossest act but existed first in thought before it took body. Without thinking, a man would go without his dinner. Every act proves a precedent thought. This is an absolute law of the mind. As all human acts pre-suppose human thought, so superhuman acts pre-suppose superhuman thought. A man is a superhuman act, and the existence of a man demonstrates the pre-existence of God.

THE END.

www.ingramcontent.com/pod-product-compliance
Lightning Source LLC
LaVergne TN
LVHW011228110826
845150LV00006B/1578

* 9 7 8 1 4 2 5 5 1 4 9 4 5 *